Artificial Intelligence

Harnessing the Power of Machine Learning and Deep Learning

Evan McCarty

Table of Contents

INTRODUCTION

In a world where technology is advancing at an astounding rate, artificial intelligence (AI), machine learning (ML), and deep learning (DL) are leading the way in bringing about previously unheard-of changes to almost every aspect of our lives. Artificial intelligence (AI) has become ingrained in modern life, from smart homes anticipating our needs to modern medical diagnostics, demonstrating its indispensable role as a partner in human progress rather than merely an aid.

With its title, "Artificial Intelligence: Harnessing the Power of Machine Learning and Deep Learning," the e-book seeks to serve as your introduction to this fascinating and ever-evolving world, where the limits of human capabilities are continually being pushed to the limit. Whether you are an experienced practitioner looking to expand your knowledge or a curious mind exploring this field for the first time, this thorough guide aims to provide insightful information.

We will go on an insightful journey together in the upcoming chapters as we examine the complex web of ideas, advancements, and technologies that make up the field of artificial intelligence. We will discuss the algorithms that enable machines to learn from and forecast data as we delve deeply into machine learning principles. As we continue, we will delve deeper and deeper into the fascinating field of deep learning, a subset of machine learning that is described by neural networks that can remarkably mimic the functioning of the human brain.

Along the way, we will also become familiar with the essential frameworks and tools that make AI solution development easier. This book aims to provide you with a comprehensive understanding of the evolving field of artificial intelligence, from discussing the ethical considerations and challenges to understanding the critical role of data.

Furthermore, it is necessary to look ahead as we are on the verge of a new era defined by the convergence of AI and quantum computing and the growing use of AI in industries such as healthcare. A future that promises not only new developments in technology but also a fresh phase of human inventiveness and resourcefulness.

Come along on this incredible journey with us as we explore the possibilities and navigate the challenges of deep learning, machine learning, and artificial intelligence. We hope this journey will provide you with the skills and knowledge required to utilize AI fully, helping shape a future in which humankind and technology work together to achieve previously unimaginable levels of development and prosperity.

Welcome to "Artificial Intelligence: Harnessing the Power of Machine Learning and Deep Learning." This is where your road to the future starts.

CHAPTER I

Basics of Artificial Intelligence

What is AI?

The word "artificial intelligence," which was formerly reserved for science fiction, is now at the forefront of technological developments influencing the contemporary world. The phrase itself piques interest and fascination since it suggests the development of intelligent machines that can carry out tasks without human intervention. These machines can mimic cognitive processes like learning and problem-solving, which were previously only possible with human intelligence. However, to fully appreciate AI's scope and depth, a more thorough understanding of its fundamental ideas, historical developments, applications, and implications for humankind's future is required.

Artificial intelligence is, at its core, a field of computer science that invloves developing machines that are capable of performing tasks that ordinarily need human intelligence. These activities cover a broad spectrum, such as comprehending natural language, identifying patterns, resolving challenging issues, and making judgments. Not only does AI aim to automate repetitive tasks, but it also promotes the creation of machines that are capable of self-improvement and can learn from mistakes in the same way that people do. To create artificial intelligence that may one day outperform human cognitive capacities, this field combines several academic fields, such as mathematics, neuroscience, linguistics, operations research, economics, and more.

When a group of forward-thinking mathematicians and scientists convened in 1956 at the Dartmouth Conference to begin exploring machine intelligence's potential, artificial intelligence started in the middle of the 20th century. This conference was the first to recognize AI as a field officially. The field experienced several ups and downs over the years, with years of increased funding and skepticism interspersed with periods of intense interest. However, the turn of the 21st century brought with it a golden age for AI, driven by breakthroughs in algorithmic design, data accessibility, and processing capacity. A subset of artificial intelligence termed machine learning has become a potent tool because it allows machines to learn and make decisions without needing to be specifically programmed to do so.

Artificial intelligence is based on the idea of algorithms, which are computer programs that computers follow to carry out tasks or solve problems. These algorithms, as they relate to artificial intelligence, are made to let computers learn from data by spotting patterns and gradually improving the accuracy of their predictions. Deep learning results from additional advancements in this field driven by the development of neural networks, which were inspired by the interconnected neuron structure in the human brain. This particular area of machine learning is concerned with analyzing different parts of data through a hierarchy of layers of algorithms, intending to possibly reveal complex patterns that are impossible for humans to notice.

Investigating artificial intelligence's diverse manifestations is necessary to comprehend how it works. Artificial General Intelligence (AGI) was the term used to describe the early perception of artificial intelligence as a system that could generalize human intelligence. Artificial general intelligence (AGI) aims to build machines with broad and flexible intelligence that can perform better than humans on almost any cognitive task. Nevertheless, the road to AGI is still very long, with most current progress focused on Narrow AI or Weak AI. Narrow AI doesn't cover the full spectrum of human cognitive capacities; instead, it focuses on executing particular tasks. Narrow artificial intelligence (AI) has advanced significantly despite its limitations, finding applications across multiple industries and transforming procedures and operations.

Artificial intelligence has slid smoothly into many facets of everyday life, frequently in ways that aren't immediately apparent. Artificial Intelligence is pervasive, from search engines that use sophisticated algorithms to deliver precise results to voice-activated assistants that assist with daily schedule management. It helps with early disease detection in the healthcare industry, improving the accuracy and efficacy of treatments. It is guiding the development of autonomous vehicles in the automotive industry, intending to create safer and more effective transportation systems in the future. AI impacts various industries, including finance, where it helps with fraud detection and risk assessment, and agriculture, where it helps with crop yield optimization through predictive analysis.

Moreover, artificial intelligence has the potential to impact the job market in the future significantly. Jobs will likely change in nature as machines gain greater capability to complete tasks that humans have historically completed. It may result in the automation of repetitive tasks, but it also creates opportunities for new positions centered around managing and collaborating with AI systems. As a result, AI promotes reevaluating skills and emphasizing the development of creativity, critical thinking, and problem-solving skills—uniquely human qualities that machines cannot replicate.

Despite its bright future, artificial intelligence is not without its difficulties and detractors. The ethical implications of AI are among the major worries it raises. Privacy and consent are raised by the use of AI in data analysis and surveillance. Furthermore, biased data can produce biased results, reinforcing preexisting societal inequalities and stereotypes. AI systems are only as good as the data fed into them. Debates concerning accountability and responsibility are also sparked by the idea of machine autonomy, particularly in situations where AI systems could harm people or make bad decisions. Therefore, as the field develops, it will be essential to guide the development and application of AI technologies through a multidisciplinary approach that considers ethical considerations.

In the future, it appears that artificial intelligence will continue to progress and be incorporated into more areas of human society. Emerging technologies such as quantum computing present the potential for greatly enhanced computational capabilities, which could usher in a new era of AI development. Future artificial intelligence seems within reach as practitioners and researchers keep pushing the envelope of what AI can accomplish, improving capabilities and promoting advancement.

In conclusion, artificial intelligence is proof of human inventiveness and the unwavering quest of knowledge and advancement. It captures the desire to push the limits of what machines are capable of doing, promoting a mutually beneficial partnership between technology and people. Artificial Intelligence has come a long way from its conception in the middle of the 20th century to its current forms. As we approach a time of unparalleled technological progress, artificial intelligence (AI) looks set to play a major role in defining the course of the future. It heralds a future in which robots will be tools and collaborators with humans, helping to create a more productive, inclusive, and thriving society.

We must approach this dynamic field with a balanced viewpoint, considering its challenges and promising future as we navigate its complexities and potential. By cultivating an environment that values creativity, cooperation, and moral reflection, we can use artificial intelligence to spark positive change and lead humanity toward a future of advancement and peace. As a result, the quest to comprehend and incorporate AI is not just a technical undertaking but also a journey through human evolution and a monument to the seemingly endless possibilities that arise from the union of human intelligence and machine intelligence.

Different types of AI: Narrow AI vs. General AI

Artificial intelligence (AI) is a fascinating topic that continuously pushes the limits of what machines can do. It may be divided into two primary categories: general AI and narrow AI. These terminologies, which define the extent and powers of AI systems, provide information about the development of AI as a field. As we go deeper into the topic, we will outline these two well-known AI subtypes, their traits, uses, and contributions to the direction of technology and human civilization.

Weak AI, sometimes known as narrow AI, is adept at doing particular jobs at a level of efficiency that frequently exceeds that of humans. This type of AI works in a set range, concentrating on a single task and being unable to transfer knowledge and abilities across different areas. Narrow artificial intelligence, to put it simply, refers to systems created to carry out specific tasks and do not contain the whole range of cognitive capacities humans do. This narrow emphasis has made narrow AI an all-encompassing force in today's technology world by facilitating its integration into a wide range of businesses and everyday applications.

An example of a classic narrow AI application is found in digital assistants, such Siri on Apple devices or Alexa on Amazon devices. Due to their speech recognition and natural language processing capabilities, these systems help users with various tasks, like answering questions and setting reminders. Nevertheless, their operation is limited by the constraints imposed by their programming; they cannot go beyond what their creators intended. Similarly, narrow artificial intelligence (AI) is used in autonomous cars in the automotive sector. These systems are quite good at handling complicated traffic situations but are limited to driving and cannot perform other tasks.

General AI, on the other hand, also referred to as Strong AI or Full AI, represents the goal of building machines that can mimic human cognitive capacities by comprehending, learning, and adapting in various contexts. This type of artificial intelligence seeks to create machines that are not only capable of carrying out any intellectual work that a human can, but also have the capacity for thought, comprehension, and creativity. The essence of general artificial intelligence (AI) is found in its ability to solve problems, think abstractly, and recognize and communicate emotions. These traits enable machines to become intelligent, but also flexible and wide-ranging.

The quest for General AI represents a significant advancement in artificial intelligence and the possibility of computers becoming self-sufficient and capable of comprehending and navigating the world's complexity like that of humans. This entails creating artificial intelligence (AI) systems that can learn and adapt over time, take in new data, and use it to make wise decisions in various situations. The ultimate form of machine intelligence is general artificial intelligence (AI), in which machines can think for themselves, comprehend their own existence, and behave in a way similar to that of human consciousness.

However, there are several conceptual and technical obstacles in the way of developing general artificial intelligence. It would be technologically impossible to create an AI system with a cognitive architecture similar to the human brain without making significant advances in computer power and algorithmic design. In terms of philosophy, it poses significant queries concerning the nature of consciousness, intelligence, and the possible ramifications of developing artificial intelligence that may one day surpass that of humans.

Within this framework, the development of artificial intelligence as a field shows a move from Narrow AI to the aspirational target of General AI. Significant progress has been created in Narrow AI thus far, with systems proving their worth in various specialized fields. Narrow AI has demonstrated the potential of machine intelligence to enhance human capabilities and promote efficiency and innovation across sectors. From AI algorithms that can beat human champions in games like Go and Chess to systems that can analyze large datasets to find patterns and make predictions.

On the other hand, while scientists and engineers struggle with the challenges of reproducing human intellect in computers, the hunt for General AI is marked by continuous research and experimentation. To create a comprehensive AI entity that can coexist peacefully with human society, this attempt involves not only the duplication of cognitive functions but also the integration of emotional and social intelligence. The quest for general artificial intelligence also raises moral issues, sparking debates about the ramifications of building sentient machines and their possible effects on society and humanity.

Moreover, the emergence of General AI indicates significant changes in the socio-economic environment since machines possessing a wide range of cognitive capacities may be able to perform a variety of tasks, which would alter the nature of the labor market and open up new opportunities for human-machine cooperation. In this sense, the development of AI raises concerns about the nature of labor, education, and the abilities needed to survive in a society where machines may collaborate with people to create a future marked by harmony and innovation.

The legislative and governance structures that would be crucial in directing the development and application of AI technologies must also be considered as we contemplate the future of artificial intelligence, especially in the context of general artificial intelligence. Artificial intelligence (AI) research must take a multidisciplinary approach that considers ethical issues, societal values, and legal frameworks since the rise of sentient computers raises questions about rights, obligations, and the potential consequences for society.

The distinction between Narrow AI and General AI acts as a road map, outlining the development of artificial intelligence as a field, at a time when technology is advancing rapidly. It's a progression, where the first steps toward reaching a machine intelligence level that mimics—and maybe even exceeds—Narrow AI represents human cognitive capacities. Throughout this journey, humanity is both the creator and the beneficiary, using AI to accelerate development and promote a future marked by creativity, cooperation, and harmony.

In conclusion, investigating the two categories of artificial intelligence—Narrow AI and General AI—provides an enlightening look at the opportunities and difficulties present in this rapidly evolving science. Through specialized applications, Narrow AI is still revolutionizing businesses and daily life; nonetheless, General AI marks the frontier of AI research, a quest to discover the mysteries of human intelligence and perhaps even a new age of technological growth. It is our duty to embark on this exploration with a feeling of duty and foresight, cultivating an innovative culture driven by moral principles and a dedication to the advancement of society.

Let's embrace the promise of artificial intelligence as a force for good as we forge ahead into the future collaboratively and inquisitively. By working together, scientists, technologists, ethicists, and the general public can successfully navigate the complexities of this rapidly developing field and steer towards a future in which artificial intelligence is recognized as a symbol of human ingenuity, a beacon of progress in the pursuit of knowledge, and a collaborator on the path to prosperity, innovation, and harmony.

Real-world applications of AI

The remarkable branch of computer science, artificial intelligence (AI), has unquestionably established itself as a key component of contemporary technological developments. Artificial intelligence (AI), manifested in various applications, has impacted every aspect of our everyday lives and changed how we see and engage with the world. AI significantly impacts every industry, including healthcare, banking, transportation, and entertainment. This has created an environment full of opportunities and potential for innovation and efficiency. It is crucial to highlight the numerous real-world AI applications that are transforming sectors and altering social standards as we move through the history of modern society.

Artificial Intelligence has become a potent tool in the healthcare industry, transforming treatment procedures and diagnostic techniques. For example, the use of AI in medical imaging has made it easier to identify illnesses early and provide prompt, potentially life-saving interventions to patients. With an accuracy that exceeds human limits, machine learning algorithms sort through enormous amounts of data to find patterns and abnormalities. AI is helping to create treatment plans specific to each patient in the field of personalized medicine. These plans consider various factors, such as genetic makeup, lifestyle, and environmental influences. This marks the beginning of a new era in proactive and personalized healthcare.

Furthermore, AI has flourished in the field of drug discovery, quickening the rate of investigation and cutting expenses related to the creation of novel medications. Artificial intelligence (AI) algorithms examine intricate biological data to find possible drug candidates and forecast their safety and efficacy profiles. This expedites the drug development process and accelerates the release of life-saving drugs. Furthermore, AI-powered virtual health assistants are advancing healthcare by bridging gaps, enabling remote monitoring and assistance, improving access to care in underserved and remote areas, and creating a more inclusive healthcare environment.

One of the main pillars of the world economy, the financial industry, has likewise welcomed AI and is using it to promote efficiency and innovation. High-frequency trading systems are controlled by AI-driven algorithms that analyze market trends and execute trades at rates faster than those of a human being, optimizing investing strategies and maximizing returns. AI has also added a new layer to risk management; machine learning models can now more accurately identify possible financial downturns, enabling preventive steps to lessen negative effects.

With the use of chatbots and virtual assistants, artificial intelligence (AI) has brought a revolutionary approach to customer service. These artificial intelligence entities can manage numerous client inquiries concurrently, offering prompt responses and resolutions, thus improving customer satisfaction and cultivating brand loyalty. These AI systems are convenient, but they also collect valuable data that can be utilized to enhance company plans and customize products to match the preferences and trends of customers.

Moving on to the domain of transportation, artificial intelligence is a precursor to a new era marked by sustainability and self-sufficiency. With the introduction of AI-powered autonomous vehicles with advanced sensors and algorithms, the urban scene will be altered, resulting in less traffic and fewer accidents brought on by mistakes made by people. These self-driving cars and advanced traffic management systems portend an efficient and ecologically friendly transportation future that will support international efforts to tackle climate change and promote sustainable development.

Furthermore, incorporating AI in the aerospace sector has promoted navigation systems and aircraft design developments, improving efficiency and safety. Large volumes of data are analyzed by AI systems, which then optimize fuel and flight routes to reduce the impact of air travel in the environment. Additionally, AI-powered robots are advancing human knowledge and promoting a deeper comprehension of the cosmos in the field of space exploration by exploring previously unexplored regions, completing tasks, and conducting research in adverse conditions.

AI has become a potent tool for content generation and delivery in the entertainment sector. Artificial intelligence (AI) algorithms examine viewership trends and preferences to personalize content recommendations that improve the viewing experience. AI is also being used to create animations and visual effects, which is encouraging fresh innovation and creativity in the entertainment industry. AI-powered non-player characters (NPCs) have also brought a new degree of intricacy and immersion to the gaming world. These NPCs have raised the bar for gaming experiences by imitating human players' actions and techniques.

Furthermore, AI enables tailored learning experiences, causing a paradigm shift in the education sector. Artificial intelligence (AI) systems examine each student's distinct learning styles and inclinations, customizing learning resources to fulfill their specific requirements and promoting a welcoming and flexible learning atmosphere. Additionally, AI is being used to create intelligent tutoring systems that give students immediate feedback and direction, improving learning and promoting academic success.

AI has sparked a revolution in agriculture that is sustainable and precision-oriented. Drones and sensors with AI capabilities track crop conditions in real time, sending back information to help farmers make educated decisions about fertilization, irrigation, and pest management. These AI systems support international initiatives to promote sustainable agriculture and food security by optimizing resource usage, cutting waste, and limiting environmental effect.

Deeper exploration of the subtleties of AI applications reveals that this marvel of technology is also finding use in the creative and artistic domains. Artificial intelligence (AI) algorithms are being utilized to produce music and artwork, opening up new creative possibilities. These artificial intelligence (AI) systems examine patterns and trends to create compositions and artworks that are both distinctive and alluring. This encourages a conversation between technology and creativity while also upending preconceived ideas about artistic authorship and innovation.

Additionally, AI is advancing communication and language translation, dismantling obstacles and promoting a global community marked by cooperation and understanding. Cross-border communication and cooperation are made easier by AI-powered translation systems that examine linguistic subtleties and context to provide accurate and culturally appropriate translations.

As we approach the dawn of a new era, it is clear that artificial intelligence (AI) has various applications that affect every aspect of human society and create an environment that is rich in possibilities and creativity. But it's also critical to approach it responsibly and strategically, considering any ethical dilemmas and potential difficulties that may arise from using AI technology. Challenges related to data security, privacy, and misuse demand the creation of strong legal frameworks that protect people's rights and the interests of society as a whole.

The spread of AI technology also begs concerns about the nature of labor in the future and the possibility of job displacement. It's essential to have a conversation about AI systems' impact on the labor market and the skills needed to keep up with the quickly changing technological landscape as these systems continue to supplement and occasionally even replace human labor. Programs for education and training must adjust in this context to support the development of skills that meet the demands of an AI-integrated and innovative future.

In conclusion, it is clear that AI is a lighthouse of advancement, a monument to human inventiveness and the never-ending quest of knowledge, as we make our way through the complexities of the modern world. Artificial Intelligence has many practical applications that are changing industries and society standards. As we approach the dawn of a new era, we must do so with responsibility and vision, encouraging an innovative culture driven by moral principles and a dedication to societal advancement. We can use AI to create a future of wealth, sustainability, and harmony by working together and taking a holistic approach. In this future, technology will act as a catalyst for positive change and a ray of hope for future generations.

CHAPTER II

Understanding Machine Learning

Definition and characteristics

Within the vast field of computational intelligence, machine learning has become a highly effective and adaptable instrument, pioneering an unparalleled transformation in engaging with the deluge of data that permeates contemporary society. The idea behind machine learning, a branch of artificial intelligence, is to give machines the capacity to learn from experiences and adjust accordingly, like how humans learn. It signifies a departure from conventional programming paradigms, where models that learn from data and get better over time take the role of explicit instructions. In order to have a deeper grasp of machine learning, it is essential to analyze its definition in detail and highlight the unique qualities that make it a powerful foundation within the field of artificial intelligence.

Fundamentally, machine learning is characterized as a data analysis technique that automates the development of analytical models. It is an interdisciplinary field that combines elements of artificial intelligence, computer science, and statistics to make algorithms that can learn from data and make predictions or judgments. The key to machine learning is the iterative nature of learning, in which the system improves its comprehension and knowledge as it is exposed to fresh data. Machine learning models can find hidden patterns and insights in data through this ongoing cycle of learning and adaptation, which helps with informed decision-making and opens up new avenues for innovative solutions to challenging issues.

One of its distinguishing features is machine learning capacity to learn independently without explicit programming to carry out a given task. The potential for autonomous learning is enabled by algorithms that learn from and become better at analyzing the data they encounter. It denotes a break from conventional programming paradigms, in which systems are created with explicit instructions in mind. Data-driven insights, where the model recognizes the underlying patterns in the data and evolves and adapts to deliver precise forecasts or solutions, are now the focus of machine learning.

The prediction accuracy attained by machine learning models is another important feature. These algorithms became skilled at spotting minute patterns and trends that could escape human examination as a result of being trained on enormous amounts of data. The predicted accuracy of the model increases with time as more data is entered into the system, enabling more sophisticated insights and well-informed decision-making. Many modern machine learning applications, such as recommendation systems in e-commerce and predictive maintenance in manufacturing, are based on this predictive ability.

Another noteworthy aspect of machine learning that merits discussion is its adaptability. Models for machine learning can be used to solve a wide range of issues in many fields and sectors. Machine learning applications are numerous and varied, ranging from healthcare (where it is utilized for personalized medication and disease prediction) to finance (where it is utilized for fraud detection systems and algorithmic trading). This adaptability results from the range of techniques and algorithms included in the machine learning domain and are appropriate for various issues and data.

Moreover, the flexibility of machine learning is what makes it so remarkable. Machine learning models can adjust to changing circumstances in a world where data is continuously changing. These models are especially well-suited to dynamic situations because they can adapt their predictions and choices in response to new input through continuous learning. This flexibility is essential in domains like cybersecurity, where machine learning models must constantly adapt to novel threats and weaknesses.

The ability of machine learning to extract and select features is another key aspect. Traditional data analysis frequently necessitates the manual identification of pertinent elements by domain specialists. Machine learning algorithms, conversely, can automatically determine which features in a dataset are most significant, which can lead to new discoveries and improve forecast accuracy. This skill creates new opportunities for comprehending complex events in addition to improving the effectiveness of the data analysis process.

Another critical aspect of machine learning models is their scalability. The capacity to examine and draw conclusions from data is becoming more and more crucial as the amount of data in the globe keeps growing exponentially. Machine learning models can handle large data sets, which can also be used to extract insightful information and support well-informed decision-making at a scale that is not achievable with more conventional analysis methods. Because of its scalability, machine learning has become a vital tool in the big data era, as businesses want to use the massive volumes of data at their disposal to obtain a competitive advantage.

It is also important to discuss how machine learning models are collaborative now. Machine learning models frequently function in concert with other systems, including other machine learning models, to offer comprehensive solutions to challenging issues rather than operating alone. Using a variety of skill sets and knowledge bases, this collaborative approach promotes innovation and makes it easier to design more reliable and efficient solutions.

It is essential to talk about the ethical issues involved in using machine learning when describing its features. It is essential to make sure that machine learning models are created and applied properly because they are frequently used to make decisions that impact people and society. The ethical implications of machine learning must be carefully considered in light of issues like data privacy, bias in machine learning models, and the possibility of misuse. Furthermore, establishing trust and encouraging a responsible attitude to the use of these technologies depends heavily on the explainability and openness of machine learning models.

In conclusion, machine learning is a dynamic and diverse discipline that encompasses a number of qualities that make it a key player in the current state of technology. It is a disruptive force in the field of artificial intelligence due to its capacity for feature extraction and scalability, as well as its ability to train on its own and have predictive accuracy, versatility, and adaptability. The growing influence of machine learning on different aspects of life is something we should be aware of and responsible for. We should also be aware of the ethical issues involved and work to create a progressive, inclusive, and innovative environment. By gaining a comprehensive comprehension of the meaning and attributes of machine learning, we may work toward utilizing its capacity to promote constructive transformation and create a future marked by harmony, wealth, and enlightenment.

ML types: Supervised, Unsupervised, and Reinforcement Learning

As we progress into the digital age, machine learning plays an increasingly important role in forming the technology we use daily. Machine learning, a well-known branch of artificial intelligence, lets computers to analyze and learn from data on their own, becoming more proficient over time. Three main categories—supervised learning, unsupervised learning, and reinforcement learning—determine how data analysis and predictive modeling are approached in the field of machine learning. These paradigms all have distinctive qualities and approaches that make it easier to create intelligent systems that can provide insightful information and solve challenging challenges. This section aims to provide a thorough understanding of these three forms of machine learning by clarifying their unique traits, approaches, and uses.

Let's start by examining the supervised learning paradigm, which functions with the assistance of labeled data. A dataset with well-defined input-output relationships is used to train the model in supervised learning. The model basically learns to translate inputs to outputs, with the ultimate goal being the capacity to make precise judgments or predictions when faced with novel, unseen data. This learning process can be compared to a student learning under a teacher's guidance, where the teacher offers the correct answers and the student gradually gains the ability to solve related issues independently.

Regression and classification are the two primary objectives in supervised learning. Predicting continuous values, like stock prices or a company's prospective growth rate, is the task of regression. However, classification is concerned with making predictions about discrete values, such as determining if an email is spam or not. Because the correctness and completeness of the training data directly affect the model's effectiveness, supervised learning methods place a high value on both the quantity and quality of the data. Supervised learning has been widely used in practice across several fields, such as sentiment analysis, credit scoring, and medical diagnosis. It is an effective tool for data analysis and predictive modeling because of its capacity to provide exact forecasts based on past data.

We leave the controlled setting of supervised learning behind and enter the world of unsupervised learning, a branch of machine learning that finds its calling in uncovering hidden structures and patterns in unlabeled data. Without a "teacher" to provide direction, unsupervised learning occurs without predetermined labels or goals. Instead, the model independently learns to recognize underlying patterns and groupings in the data. Finding hidden structures and insights that are not immediately obvious is the main goal here in order to help gain a deeper comprehension of the intrinsic properties of the data.

Within the field of unsupervised learning, there exist various methodologies and approaches, such as clustering and association. By putting data points with comparable characteristics together, a process known as clustering makes it easier to spot patterns and trends in the dataset. On the other hand, association focuses on identifying patterns in a database that show connections between seemingly unrelated pieces of information. These methods allow unsupervised learning to uncover new insights and support data-driven decision-making across a range of domains, such as network security anomaly detection and market and customer segmentation. For exploratory data analysis and knowledge discovery, unsupervised learning is essential because it evaluates complicated data without predefined labels.

Further exploring the field of machine learning, we come across the dynamic paradigm of reinforcement learning, which has its roots in behavioral psychology. Reinforcement learning focuses on creating agents that can interact with their surroundings to accomplish tasks or optimize a concept of cumulative reward. The agent learns to make decisions by interacting with the environment and getting feedback in the form of rewards or penalties. This trial-and-error method of learning is what makes this process unique. The ultimate goal is to create a policy that directs the agent to pursue acts that maximize the cumulative reward over time.

Reinforcement learning sets itself apart by emphasizing sequential decision-making and taking the challenge as a whole into account rather than breaking it down into smaller jobs. Its foundations are in control theory and dynamic programming, and it includes a broad range of techniques and algorithms that make it easier to create intelligent agents that can learn behaviors that are either optimal or nearly optimal. Reinforcement learning finds wide-ranging applications in fields such as robotics, where agents are trained to navigate intricate surroundings, and game play, where agents are taught methods to win games. Reinforcement learning is a potent method for creating systems that can adjust and improve their behavior over time because of its emphasis on learning through interaction.

It is clear from analyzing these machine learning paradigms that they all have unique traits and methods of learning. With its focus on labeled data, supervised learning offers an organized method for predictive modeling that makes accurate predictions and judgments based on past data possible. Unsupervised learning provides an avenue for exploratory data analysis and knowledge discovery because of its capacity to reveal hidden structures and patterns in data. Reinforcement learning emphasizes interaction and feedback to help construct intelligent agents that can adjust and optimize their behavior in changing contexts.

We must use these machine learning paradigms to promote creativity and constructive change as we approach the dawn of a new era of technological growth. Combining the advantages of supervised, unsupervised, and reinforcement learning, hybrid models that integrate different learning paradigms can be developed more easily, opening the door to more reliable and efficient solutions to challenging issues.

In conclusion up, the domain of machine learning is a dynamic and constantly changing field, characterized by the persistent introduction of novel approaches, procedures, and uses. As we go deeper into this field, we discover that reinforcement learning, supervised learning, and unsupervised learning are the three pillars supporting machine learning structure, each offering special insights and methods for predictive modeling and data analysis. By gaining a sophisticated comprehension of these learning paradigms, we can strive to create intelligent systems that will improve our comprehension of the world and help create a future characterized by efficiency, innovation, and wealth.

Key algorithms and their applications

Machine learning, a multidisciplinary topic that integrates aspects of artificial intelligence, statistics, and computer science, occupies a special place in the current digital era that is defined by automated decision-making and data-driven insights. In this quest, the algorithms that form the foundation of machine learning systems play a crucial role. These algorithms, distinguished by their computational effectiveness and mathematical rigor, make extracting insightful information from large, complicated data sets easier. A thorough investigation of these algorithms and the plethora of uses for which they may be put to good use promises to be both an intellectual journey into the field of machine learning and a window into the future of technological advancement. This section aims to outline some of the fundamental algorithms that underpin machine learning systems and provide a thorough analysis of the numerous ways in which they are used in modern society.

We start by looking at the Linear Regression technique, which is a basic tool used in statistical analysis and predictive modeling. A linear relationship between a variable that is dependent and one or more independent variables is the goal of linear regression, one of the most basic and popular algorithms. It can forecast the dependent variable's result based on the values of the independent variables by determining this relationship. Because of its adaptability and ease of use, linear regression has been used extensively in various fields, including business, healthcare, and economics. As a result, it is now considered an essential tool for machine learning practitioners, with applications ranging from sales forecasting to disease progression prediction and economic trend prediction.

As we follow the path of linear models, we come across the classification process known as logistic regression, which is really employed to predict a categorical dependent variable. This technique is highly appropriate for binary classification problems like spam identification in email filtering systems or customer churn prediction in marketing analytics, as it calculates the likelihood that a given input point belongs to a specific category. It is a preferred option for applications that need a detailed grasp of the underlying probabilistic relationships within the data because of its probabilistic foundation and computing performance.

When one delves further into the field of machine learning, one finds that Decision Trees are a potent family of algorithms that can be applied to tasks involving both regression and classification. These algorithms work by dividing the data into subsets according to the input feature values, resulting in a decision tree-like model. Decision trees are commonly used in many industries, including manufacturing for quality control procedures, finance for credit risk assessment, and medicine for diagnostic systems due to their ease of use and interpretability. Moreover, ensemble approaches like Random Forests expand decision trees' capabilities, which construct many decision trees and combine their predictions. This results in more accurate and reliable models that can handle complicated, high-dimensional data.

Further exploration reveals Support Vector Machines (SVM) as a class of algorithms distinguished by their robustness and mathematical elegance. The main application of SVMs is in classification tasks; in these cases, they identify the hyperplane in the feature space that best divides the classes. SVMs provide a versatile and effective method for solving classification issues. They can also handle non-linearly separable data by utilizing kernel functions. SVMs are used in many different fields, including text mining for sentiment analysis, image recognition for object detection, and bioinformatics for protein classification. These applications demonstrate how adaptable and powerful SVMs are for solving challenging classification issues.

The K-means clustering algorithm is a often employed method in unsupervised learning to divide a data set into K unique, non-overlapping subgroups or clusters. K-means groups comparable data points together to make data analysis and visualization easier while revealing hidden structures and patterns in the data. It has a wide range of uses, from picture compression in computer vision to customer segmentation in marketing analytics, where it minimizes the number of colors in an image while maintaining its general structure and appearance.

It is impossible to disregard the significant influence of neural networks, especially Deep Learning models, which have completely transformed the area of artificial intelligence, as we make our way through the maze-like world of machine learning algorithms. These algorithms build a complex network of interconnected nodes, or "neurons," that cooperate to learn from data. The structure and operation of the human brain inspires them. Deep Learning models are especially well-suited to applications like picture and speech recognition, natural language processing, and autonomous vehicle navigation because they can learn hierarchical representations of data. The transformational potential of machine learning technologies has been demonstrated by the flood of innovation and breakthroughs that have been sparked by their unrivaled capacity to extract detailed patterns from enormous amounts of data.

The birth of Reinforcement Learning algorithms, which aim to optimize an agent's sequential decision-making process when interacting with its environment, coincides with the development of these methods. Advanced algorithms like Q-learning and Deep Q Networks (DQNs) have made it possible to create intelligent systems that can interact and receive feedback to learn the best possible strategy. Algorithms have demonstrated their mastery of sophisticated games such as Go and Poker in the gaming industry, demonstrating the strength of reinforcement learning and contributing to significant advancements in artificial intelligence.

It is clear from considering the wide range of algorithms and their uses that machine learning is characterized by a rich tapestry of techniques and strategies that make data analysis and predictive modeling easier. These algorithms, which are distinguished by their computational effectiveness and mathematical rigor, have applications in many different fields, stimulating creativity and encouraging a data-driven approach to problem-solving. The applications of these algorithms are wide-ranging and diverse, demonstrating the revolutionary potential of machine learning technology. Examples of these applications include autonomous navigation in robotics and predictive analytics in healthcare.

In conclusion, the field of machine learning is alive and well, driven by a variety of algorithms that are always changing and adjusting to the problems that the world's growing complexity presents. These algorithms—whether deep learning models or simple linear regression—offer a window into the technology of the future, where data-driven insights and automated decision-making processes can transform how we solve problems and innovate completely. In order to prepare for a future characterized by creativity, efficiency, and wealth, it is imperative that we deeply examine these algorithms as we stand on the brink of this technological revolution. By doing so, we may cultivate a sophisticated grasp of their functions and uses.

CHAPTER III

Diving Deeper into Deep Learning

What sets Deep Learning apart?

The emergence of deep learning is a significant turning point in the history of technology, marking the beginning of a new era in which intelligent machines are able to execute tasks with a level of accuracy and sophistication that often equals or exceeds that of human beings. A branch of AI and ML that has attracted much interest and funding because of its potential to bring revolutionary improvements in various fields and sectors, is known as deep learning. However, what about deep learning makes it stand out in the wide and complex field of artificial intelligence? This section seeks to explore the depths of deep learning, highlighting its distinctive features, approaches, and transformative potential that distinguish it in the rapidly developing field of artificial intelligence.

Neural networks, and especially deep neural networks—which are distinguished by their layered topologies made up of numerous interconnected nodes or neurons—are the foundation of deep learning. The neural networks seen in the human brain, where a vast number of neurons cooperate to process information and make decisions, served as the model for these structures. Because of the layered architecture of a deep learning model, data can be represented hierarchically, with lower levels learning basic patterns and higher layers building on these foundations to learn increasingly complex patterns. Deep learning is distinct from other machine learning algorithms in that it can learn hierarchical representations. This feature enables it to perform very well in applications like speech and image recognition, where the capacity to recognize and understand complicated patterns is critical.

Feature learning, sometimes referred to as representation learning, is the extraordinary capacity of deep learning models to autonomously extract features from unprocessed data. When using traditional machine learning methods, experts must frequently manually extract significant features from the data by identifying and extracting them before putting the features into the model. This limits the model's capacity to learn intricate patterns and requires a significant amount of time and work. On the other hand, deep learning models are better at automatically extracting the most relevant characteristics from unprocessed data, which improves their capacity to discover complex relationships and patterns within the data. Deep learning stands out due to the automation of feature extraction, which makes it easier to create models that are effective and potent.

The capacity of deep learning to efficiently handle enormous volumes of data is another unique feature. In today's data-rich world, the ability to evaluate and draw conclusions from huge datasets is an invaluable skill. Deep learning models are data-hungry and generally perform better the more data they are exposed to. In fields like big data analytics and data mining, where deep learning models can comb through enormous datasets to identify insightful patterns, this scalability is especially helpful. Deep learning models can now process larger datasets more quickly and effectively compared to traditional machine learning algorithms thanks to the development of specialized hardware like Graphics Processing Units (GPUs) and increased computational power.

Additionally, deep learning has proven to be incredibly adept at unsupervised learning, which is the process by which a model learns to recognize hidden structures and patterns in unlabeled data. Deep learning may produce new data samples that are similar to a given dataset using methods like deep generative models, which promotes improvements in areas like text-to-speech synthesis and image production. These capabilities have sparked innovation across a range of fields, such as the production of lifelike virtual assistants that can interact naturally with humans and realistic computer-generated images for use in motion pictures.

Additionally, transfer learning—where previously trained models can be adjusted to complete new tasks with less data—is an area in which deep learning shines. Because deep learning can transfer information from one task to another, it can be used as a versatile tool in the construction of intelligent systems, reducing the requirement for huge volumes of labeled data and processing resources. Because of its superiority in transfer learning, deep learning models have been quickly used in a variety of applications, like natural language processing systems in intelligent assistants and computer vision systems in autonomous cars.

Deep learning has the ability to revolutionize many fields, sparking a wave of creativity and upheaval. Deep learning models are being used in healthcare to analyze medical images more accurately than professional radiologists, enabling the early diagnosis of diseases. Deep learning is used in the automobile industry to fuel autonomous vehicles' vision systems, which allow them to safely and effectively navigate challenging environments. Deep learning has made it easier to create complex language models in the field of natural language processing that can comprehend and produce writing that is similar to that of a human, creating new opportunities for automated content production, sentiment analysis, and machine translation.

Deep learning has numerous advantages, but it also has drawbacks. Deep learning models are complicated, which frequently means that they require more resources and incur large computational costs. Furthermore, these models' interpretability problems arise in fields where explainability and transparency are essential. Moreover, deep learning models can overfit, particularly when trained on sparse data, which could lead to models that are not very good at generalizing to new, unseen data. To overcome these obstacles, more research and development is required to improve deep learning systems' effectiveness and efficiency.

In conclusion, deep learning is an innovative approach to artificial intelligence that is distinguished by its multilayer neural networks, automated feature extraction, and ability to handle massive amounts of data. Its revolutionary potential is visible in a wide range of businesses, where it is propelling developments in autonomous navigation, language interpretation, and medical diagnostics, among other fields. The ability of deep learning to learn hierarchical data representations is what really makes it unique; it allows for the creation of models that comprehend and interpret complicated patterns with an artificial intelligence level of sophistication and depth that is unmatched. Deep learning is a promising sign of intelligent machines that will enhance our comprehension of the world and usher in a new era of innovation and progress as we traverse the rapidly changing digital terrain.

Neural networks: the backbone of DL

In a world where technology is advancing at an accelerating rate, artificial intelligence (AI) has become the center of invention and discovery. The idea of deep

36

learning (DL), a machine learning method that is changing businesses, altering research paradigms, and promoting a new era of intelligent systems, is fundamental to this explosion in AI advancements. Neural networks are a complex and intriguing field that form the basis of deep learning, providing the conceptual and computational frameworks necessary for the process. This section aims to explore the intricacies and subtleties of neural networks, clarifying their function as the foundation of deep learning and investigating the principles that make them an effective tool in today's computer environment.

One must first investigate the history and underlying theories of neural networks in order to comprehend the critical role that these networks play in deep learning. Inspired by the biological neural networks that form the animal brains, neural networks are collections of algorithms that aim to identify underlying links in a dataset by simulating the functioning of the human brain. With this biomimetic approach to machine learning, computer models that can learn, reason, and adapt like their biological counterparts are becoming more prevalent. A neural network's primary function is to mimic the interconnected neuron nodes seen in the human brain. This allows the system to examine and decipher intricate patterns and relationships found in data sets.

In a typical neural network, information is processed and transmitted by a multiplicity of interconnected nodes, or neurons, arranged into layers. Three different types of layers typically make up a network: the input layer, which receives the initial data; the hidden layers, which process the data using weighted connections; and the output layer, which generates the prediction or final result. To reduce the error between the expected and actual outputs, the weight and bias assigned to each neuron in these layers are adjusted during training. Neural networks are capable to learn and model intricate, non-linear interactions because of this layered, hierarchical structure, which paves the way for the creation of complicated deep learning models.

It is impossible to investigate the field of neural networks without studying the intricate learning algorithms and procedures that these networks are built upon. The capacity of neural networks to learn and adapt is one of its most important features; backpropagation is a technique that makes this possible. The network optimizes the network's performance over time via backpropagating, which modifies the weights and biases of neurons based on the gradient of the loss function. By repeating forward and backward runs, the network may learn intricate patterns and relationships from the data, which makes it easier to create strong and accurate models. Optimization techniques like gradient descent, which aim to minimize the loss function and guide the network towards optimal performance, further improve the learning process.

We come across a variety of architectures as we go further into the field of neural networks, each having special traits and uses. The most basic kind of neural network, feedforward neural networks, do not have cycles or loops; instead, data flows directly from the input layer to the output layer. Recurrent Neural Networks (RNNs) are a popular tool in time series prediction and natural language processing, but they also handle sequential data very well since they add loops to allow for information persistence. Similar to this, convolutional layers—which allow convolutional neural networks (CNNs) to automatically and adaptively learn the spatial hierarchies of features from input images—have completely changed the area of computer vision.

The essential building blocks of deep learning are neural networks, an expansive and ever-changing field that facilitates the creation of intelligent systems with independent learning and reasoning abilities. They are effective tools for the study and interpretation of big, complicated data sets because of their capacity to learn hierarchical representations of data, automatically extract features, and model intricate, non-linear relationships. This has sparked a wave of creative applications that span from autonomous cars, where neural networks enable the development of complex vision systems capable of navigating the complexities of the real world, to medical image analysis, where they aid in the detection and diagnosis of diseases.

Furthermore, there is a culture of constant innovation and research in the field of neural networks, which encourages the creation of innovative models and architectures that push the envelope of what is feasible. Generative Adversarial Networks (GANs) are a relatively new concept in machine learning. Essentially, two networks—a discriminator and a generator—cooperate to produce new data samples that have similarities to a given dataset. These networks have shown the adaptability and potential of neural networks in promoting innovation and advancement in a variety of sectors, such as image generation, style transmission, and data augmentation.

However, the neural network journey is not without its difficulties. Deep neural network training frequently takes a significant amount of time and processing power, especially as the network's complexity rises. Furthermore, there are questions about openness and reliability due to the "black box" character of these networks, where the internal workings are not entirely understood or interpretable. Moreover, neural networks can overfit—a phenomenon in which they absorb the noise present in the training set and hence perform poorly when applied to fresh, untrained data. These difficulties call for a concentrated effort in research and development to improve neural networks' robustness, efficiency, and transparency.

With artificial intelligence and data-driven insights ushering in a new era, neural networks become a shining example of innovation and advancement. As the foundation of deep learning, their capacity to discover intricate patterns and relationships in data, together with their adaptability and agility, is driving a revolution in artificial intelligence. We are positioned to fully utilize neural networks due to our evolving understanding of their capabilities, opening the door to a world where intelligent machines will be able to enhance human potential and usher in a new era of creativity and discovery.

In summary, neural networks are the major components of deep learning because of their varied architectures, learning algorithms, and hierarchical structures. Their ability to learn and model intricate relationships, along with their biomimetic approach, puts them at the vanguard of the artificial intelligence revolution, propelling technological developments and igniting a new era of intelligent systems. In order to prepare for a future distinguished by creativity, effectiveness, and prosperity, it is imperative that we further our understanding of neural networks by delving deeply into their study and developing a sophisticated comprehension of their functioning and potential.

Types of Deep Learning: CNNs, RNNs, GANs, etc.

The field of artificial intelligence has experienced a remarkable explosion in recent years, primarily because of the progress made in deep learning, a branch of machine learning that has expanded our ability to create predictive models with greater accuracy. Convolutional neural networks (or CNNs), recurrent neural networks (or RNNs), and generative adversarial networks (or GANs), among other deep learning architectures, are at the core of this rapidly developing field. Each offers special features and uses that are reshaping the modern technological environment. This section seeks to explore the unique qualities of these many forms of deep learning, clarifying their nuances and demonstrating how they are leading the way in the ongoing revolution in artificial intelligence.

A class of deep learning models that have altered the field of recognition of images and videos is known as CNNs. CNNs are able to automatically and adaptively learn spatial hierarchies of features from visual data. This ability was initially sparked by the biological processes seen in the human visual cortex. A CNN often consists of several layers, such as fully connected, pooling, and convolutional layers. Convolution is the method through which the convolutional layers use filters or kernels to scan the incoming data and find patterns and features. Pooling layers come next, which minimize computing complexity while concentrating on the most important features by reducing the spatial dimensions of the data. The extracted features are eventually used by the fully connected layers to carry out classification tasks. By using a multi-layered method, CNNs can identify intricate patterns in visual data, which makes them an effective tool for computer vision applications such as autonomous car technology and facial recognition.

The development of Recurrent Neural Networks (RNNs), which have had a huge impact on the processing of sequential and time-series data, is another important turning point in the deep learning field. RNNs are distinguished by their capacity to store information about past inputs in the hidden layers of the network, creating a sort of "memory" that records information about computations made thus far. They excel at tasks like speech recognition, language modeling, and time-series prediction because of this special quality. The Long Short-Term Memory (or LSTM) network is a well-known RNN variation that incorporates gates to control the flow of information to be retained or forgotten at each time step, hence reducing the problems associated with long-term dependencies, which are a common issue in normal RNNs. RNNs and their derivatives provide a strong foundation for addressing challenging issues in audio analysis, natural language processing, and other fields where sequential data is essential.

We come across Generative Adversarial Networks (GANs), a unique and fascinating class of artificial intelligence algorithms, as we continue exploring the deep learning environment. Essentially, GANs are made up of two neural networks: a discriminator and a generator. The discriminator tries to tell the difference between generated and genuine data, while the generator aims to create data that is as similar to real data as possible. The generation of extremely realistic generated data is encouraged by these competitive dynamics, opening up a wide range of applications such as data augmentation, image generation, and art creation. The GANs have posed philosophical queries on the nature of creativity and the possibility of machines imitating human-like creative processes in addition to opening up new directions in the realm of artificial intelligence.

As we explore more, we discover that deep learning is not limited to these particular architectures. Further adorning the terrain are variations like Sequence to Sequence (Seq2Seq) models, Modular Neural Networks, and Radial Basis Function Networks (RBFNs), each of which offers distinct functionality and viewpoints. For example, RBFNs can simulate complex and non-linear relationships in data because they are very good at function approximation and interpolation tasks. They achieve this by using radial basis functions as activation functions. Similar to this, Seq2Seq models have become highly successful tools for text summarization and machine translation by effectively mapping sequences to sequences through the use of encoder-decoder architectures.

These varied architectures that make up the deep learning world are evidence of the quick advances and breakthroughs occurring in the field of artificial intelligence. With their own features and functions, each of these networks helps to broaden the scope of machine learning and usher in a new era of intelligent systems that are able to solve complicated problems on their own and learn on their own. Due to their flexibility and adaptability, they have played a significant role in advancing a number of industries, such as healthcare (where they help with medical picture processing and disease diagnosis) and the automobile (where they help with the development of autonomous driving systems).

But the road to deep learning is not without its difficulties and complexity. These networks require a significant amount of processing power and time to train, especially as the models become more intricate and detailed. To further complicate matters, choosing the right architectures, minimizing problems like overfitting and data bias, and fine-tuning these networks are all important steps towards reaching peak performance. Furthermore, a careful and responsible approach to the creation and implementation of GANs is required due to the ethical implications of deep learning, especially in light of their capacity to produce realistic-looking fake content.

In conclusion, deep learning, which is defined by the complex architectures of CNNs, RNNs, GANs, and other models, is a dynamic and developing field that is constantly pushing the limits of artificial intelligence and promoting a revolution in computational power. These networks, with their intricate hierarchies and learning processes, are influencing the direction of machine learning, adaptation, and innovation. This could lead to the discovery of previously untapped capacity in human potential and technology advancement. Now that this exciting new era is about to begin, it is critical that we explore and study these deep learning types in depth in order to develop a more nuanced understanding of their potential and workings, as well as to guide innovation toward a future characterized by intelligence, efficiency, and prosperity.

DL in action: Real-world applications

A subfield of machine learning that has become widely used in many real-world applications in the modern period, moving beyond the boundaries of theoretical research is known as deep learning. Inspired by the complex processes of the human brain, this computational technique enables machines to learn from and analyze complicated data structures, leading to unmatched improvements in a variety of industries, such as healthcare, entertainment, finance, and transportation. In this section, we examine the various domains in which deep learning has proven to be effective, providing an overview of a future in which artificial intelligence would be effortlessly incorporated into and improved upon our everyday lives.

Deep learning has become a potent tool in the healthcare industry, improving customized medicine, predictive analytics, and diagnostics. Convolutional neural networks (or CNNs), a subset of deep learning algorithms, are becoming increasingly popular among healthcare professionals for medical picture processing. These networks perform exceptionally well, often outperforming human experts in recognising patterns and abnormalities in medical images like MRIs, CT scans, and X-rays. By evaluating enormous patient data sets, deep learning has the ability to forecast the course of diseases and customize treatment regimens, ushering in a new era of precision medicine. Furthermore, deep learning models have proven crucial in the fight against global health crises by helping to analyze molecular structures in order to aid in the development of new medications and vaccinations, which could hasten the rate of scientific research and innovation.

The transportation and autonomous vehicle industries are prime examples of deep learning's transformational potential. Advanced deep learning algorithms form the core of autonomous driving systems, allowing cars to see and comprehend their environment, make data-driven judgments, and maneuver through challenging situations effectively and safely. These vehicles employ deep neural networks to process and interpret massive volumes of data in real-time, enabling responsive and adaptive driving behaviors. They do this by combining sensors, cameras, and LIDAR technologies. Deep learning is leading a revolution in transportation, offering safer and more sustainable urban mobility in the future through improving vehicle safety and possibly cutting emissions and traffic congestion.

The introduction of deep learning technologies has also caused a paradigm change in the entertainment sector. Deep learning algorithms have made it easier to create incredibly realistic and immersive settings in video games, which has greatly improved the gaming experience. Deep learning is also used in the film industry for visual effects and animations, where algorithms are able to produce remarkably accurate human face expressions, realistic lighting, and textures. Algorithms such as Generative Adversarial Networks (or GANs) are being used in the music business to write new songs, providing artists with new tools to experiment and develop.

The finance industry is not immune to the revolutionary effects of deep learning in a world where information is the new currency. Deep learning algorithms are being used more and more by financial institutions and investment businesses for risk assessment, market research, and predictive analytics. Large and intricate datasets are analyzed by these algorithms, which then identify minute patterns and trends that might provide information about the actions of the market and investment tactics. Deep learning has also aided in the development of fraud detection systems, which are now able to recognize unusual transactions and possibly reduce financial crimes with more precision and effectiveness.

The introduction of deep learning into the fields of communications and language has been nothing short of transformational. Deep learning models play a major role in Natural Language Processing (NLP), a science that connects artificial intelligence with human language. NLP tasks include sentiment analysis, text summarization, and language translation. A major improvement in human-machine interactions is the appearance of chatbots and virtual assistants, which are able to comprehend and reply to human language with increasing sophistication. Deep learning models have also made great progress in speech recognition, opening the door for voice-activated devices and interfaces that have the potential to completely change how we interact with technology.

Significant breakthroughs in security and surveillance have been brought about by deep learning. Deep learning algorithms-driven facial recognition technologies can now accurately identify people in a variety of challenging situations, including crowded and complicated ones. Analogously, these algorithms support anomaly detection, spotting odd patterns or actions in video recordings, which may improve security protocols and promote safer neighborhoods.

However, given that we are at the beginning of this new frontier, it is imperative that we proceed responsibly and cautiously. There are several ethical issues and difficulties when deep learning algorithms are used in practical applications. A careful approach to the development and use of deep learning technologies is required due to concerns about data privacy, consent, and the possibility of misuse or bias in AI systems. As such, it is our responsibility to cultivate a dialogue that promotes responsible AI, guaranteeing that the developments in this area are consistent with the more general objectives of social welfare and ethical conduct.

In conclusion, deep learning is a shining example of innovation and promise in the contemporary world, with applications spanning numerous industries and drastically altering the course of our everyday existence. Deep learning algorithms are permeating every aspect of modern life, from healthcare to entertainment, banking to transportation, and providing a window into a world of expanded capabilities and intelligent systems. It is essential that we tackle this changing environment with an exploratory and curious mindset while firmly establishing our ethical and responsible foundations. Although the field of deep learning is still in its early stages, what we can see so far offers hope for a future in which artificial intelligence will be used to maximize human potential and promote an inventive, productive, and prosperous society.

CHAPTER IV

Tools and Frameworks

Introduction to popular frameworks: TensorFlow, PyTorch, Keras, etc.

Strong and adaptable frameworks are essential as we move toward a future in which machine learning and artificial intelligence (AI) drive technological advancement. The foundation of AI and deep learning projects is formed by frameworks like TensorFlow, PyTorch, and Keras, which give developers, data scientists, and researchers the necessary tools and libraries to make the creation, training, and implementation of intricate neural network models easier. This section explores the complex world of these widely used frameworks, providing a basic overview of their features, functions, and crucial role in deep learning and artificial intelligence advancement.

Developed by Google Brain, TensorFlow is an open-source framework that is leading this technological revolution. Ever since its launch, TensorFlow has been one of the most often employed deep learning frameworks, valued for its adaptability, scalability, and large community support. TensorFlow, which is based on the concepts of data flow graphs, makes it possible to visualize and optimize intricate computational operations, creating a welcoming environment for both novices and specialists. The flexibility of TensorFlow to support both high-level and low-level APIs, accommodating users with different degrees of experience, is one of its most notable advantages. Its high-level APIs, like Keras, offer intuitive abstractions and interfaces that make neural network model construction and deployment quick and easy. However, its low-level APIs provide a fine-grained control over model structures, allowing the development of custom, complex models that meet the demands of particular projects or lines of inquiry.

The capabilities of TensorFlow are not limited to a particular field. It has significant uses in many different domains, such as time-series analysis, picture and video recognition, text-based applications, voice and speech recognition, and more. No matter the size of the project, TensorFlow's adaptability is demonstrated by its support for a variety of hardware platforms, such as CPUs, GPUs, and TPUs. This allows for high performance and efficient computing. Additionally, TensorFlow expands its capabilities into the embedded and mobile space via TensorFlow Lite, a low-cost on-device inference solution. TensorFlow is embracing a community-driven approach as it develops, creating a thriving ecosystem where researchers and developers work together to drive breakthroughs and discoveries.

The AI Research lab at Facebook has built PyTorch, a deep learning framework that is becoming a formidable competitor. Because it uses a dynamic computation graph—also referred to as the define-by-run scheme—instead of TensorFlow's define-and-run method, PyTorch has become quite popular, especially among researchers. This feature of PyTorch makes it possible to write code in a more pythonic and intuitive manner, which makes debugging simpler and the switch between Python and neural network scripting more fluid. In addition, TorchScript—an intermediate representation of a PyTorch model—is one of the many tools and features that PyTorch provides. It is used to optimize and serialize models for production deployment.

The fundamental attraction of PyTorch lies in its imperative programming paradigm, which creates a setting in which calculations are handled in real time, improving usability and allowing for dynamic training modifications. Because of this, PyTorch is especially well-suited for research and experimental projects, where adaptability and incremental improvements are essential. Additionally, PyTorch has strong support for GPU acceleration, which guarantees flexible and highly efficient computations, speeding up research and development. PyTorch is a platform that allows academics to easily experiment, iterate, and construct deep learning models. As it grows, it provides an environment that is conducive to creativity.

An interface for the TensorFlow library and a high-level neural networks API that sits at the intersection of simplicity and functionality is known as Keras. Originally designed as an intuitive API for neural network construction, Keras has developed into one of the most widely used deep learning frameworks, especially among novices due to its user-friendliness. Its streamlined approach to model creation lowers the barrier to entry for beginners to the deep learning area by making the process of generating and deploying neural networks relatively simple through the use of simple APIs and pre-defined layers.

With a focus on user experience and a suite of capabilities aimed at streamlining the development process, Keras sets itself apart. Because of its modular architecture, networks can be put together quickly and easily for both novices and specialists. Users can select from pre-built building blocks or custom components. In addition, Keras supports a variety of backend engines, giving users the freedom to select the one that best fits their project's needs, such as TensorFlow, Theano, and Microsoft Cognitive Toolkit. Deeper integration between TensorFlow and Keras keeps fostering an environment where developers may more easily and efficiently build and deploy deep learning models.

It's clear that the framework market is dynamic and ever-changing as we go farther into the fields of artificial intelligence and deep learning. In addition to TensorFlow, PyTorch, and Keras, a number of other frameworks are also making significant contributions to this dynamic ecosystem. These include Microsoft Cognitive Toolkit (CNTK), a commercial-grade toolkit that provides incredibly effective and scalable deep learning model training, and Caffe, a deep learning framework created by the Berkeley Vision and Learning Center (BVLC). These frameworks, each with its own special qualities and skills, add to a rich and varied atmosphere that fosters creativity and pushes the bounds of what is practical in the field of artificial intelligence.

But as the landscape changes, there are new issues and things to take into account. An important factor in determining a deep learning project's effectiveness, scalability, and success is the framework selection. As a result, developers and researchers need to exercise caution when navigating this environment, taking into account many aspects like the project's complexity, hardware compatibility, community support, and domain-specific requirements. Moreover, as the area develops, interoperability and standards are becoming increasingly important, encouraging partnerships and integrations that have the potential to expand these frameworks' functionality.

In conclusion, the ever-changing area of deep learning frameworks—which is exemplified by TensorFlow, PyTorch, and Keras—is evidence of the quick advances and breakthroughs that are taking place in artificial intelligence. These frameworks give the fundamental tools and libraries needed to navigate the intricate world of neural networks, each with a distinctive combination of features and capabilities. At this critical juncture in history, when artificial intelligence has the potential to fundamentally alter our surroundings, these frameworks serve as cornerstones, encouraging a culture of creativity, investigation, and advancement. Through the provision of tools to construct, train, and implement advanced neural network models, these frameworks are facilitating the advancement of humankind toward a future in which artificial intelligence enhances human capabilities and presents previously unseen prospects for development, advancement, and innovation.

As we explore more of this fascinating field, we may look forward to a time when these frameworks keep developing, incorporating new tools and techniques and encouraging a lively, cooperative community where the quest of knowledge and creativity is unrestricted. In this bright and promising future, human creativity and technological advancement will usher in a new era of artificial intelligence, motivated by the unwavering quest for advancement and the desire to realize the full potential of machine intelligence.

Selecting the right tools for the task

A key factor in success in the quickly changing field of artificial intelligence is choosing the appropriate tools for a given task. Initially, the abundance of accessible tools and frameworks could appear daunting, particularly considering the rapid rate of advancements in the domain. Professionals, researchers, and enthusiasts all find themselves sifting through a plethora of possibilities in this complex environment, trying to choose which tools would best fit their goals—whether they be related to research, development, or the implementation of AI systems. Through an exploration of the subtleties and factors that influence the process of choosing the appropriate tools for the job at hand, this section aims to provide a critical eye on this crucial facet of AI implementation.

It is critical to comprehend the depth and intricacy of the current task. There are several different subfields within artificial intelligence, each with unique requirements and complications. Artificial Intelligence encompasses a wide range of fields, including robots, computer vision, natural language processing, deep learning, and machine learning. Thus, a thorough examination of the project's goals and scope is the first stage in the tool selection process. A thorough comprehension of the issue domain can act as a compass, pointing professionals in the direction of tools that provide features that meet the requirements of their projects.

Furthermore, the knowledge and abilities of the project management team have a big impact on the process of choosing the appropriate tools. In the field of artificial intelligence, where technologies can be as simple as they are complicated, the team's technical expertise is a critical factor. Higher level of abstraction tools, like Keras, can be a good fit for teams who are just starting to learn about AI because they have a more gradual learning curve and can help jumpstart projects more quickly. However, frameworks that provide fine-grained control over model topologies, like TensorFlow or PyTorch, may be the better option for teams that are well-versed in the nuances of artificial intelligence. This allows for the development of complex and unique solutions.

Alongside the assessment of skill sets, the project's characteristics have a major impact on the selection procedure. Dynamic computation graphs, a feature of frameworks like as PyTorch, are useful for research-oriented projects, which typically include experimentation and iterative advancements. On the other hand, frameworks like TensorFlow, which are renowned for their high efficiency and scalability characteristics, may prove to be a dependable ally for production-focused projects where scalability and performance are critical. Therefore, a sophisticated comprehension of the project's focus, be it production or research, can act as a lighthouse, directing tool selection in the direction of instruments that enhance project dynamics.

Another crucial consideration in the choosing process is the programming language of choice. The choice of language can have a big impact on the tools that are used because there is such a wide variety of languages accessible, including Python, R, Java, and others. Python is a well-liked option in the AI community because of its extensive library ecosystem and strong community. Tools and frameworks that operate well with Python may make development easier and create an atmosphere where writing and implementation are done in a more efficient manner.

Furthermore, the choice of tools may also be influenced by the hardware infrastructure that is in place. The degree to which different frameworks are compatible with different hardware configurations—such as CPUs, GPUs, and TPUs—varies. Tools that support GPUs or TPUs can be helpful in situations when high-performance computation is required. This allows for faster computations and, consequently, a quicker turnaround time for project milestones. Therefore, a crucial part of the decision process should involve taking into account both possible hardware improvements and the current hardware infrastructure.

Documentation and community support are two more pillars in the tool selection process. A strong community can be a great advantage since it offers a forum for cooperation, knowledge sharing, and problem-solving. Active communities support tools that can provide a more comprehensive development experience by opening up opportunities for learning and improvement. Moreover, thorough documentation may be a dependable partner during the development process, providing direction, advice, and support for troubleshooting as needed.

Cost factors are also important to take into account. While a large number of AI frameworks and tools are free and available to the public, others may have additional expenses such as licensing. A review of the project budget and an analysis of the possible return on investment might be important components of the selection process. Tools that strike an appropriate balance between functionality and affordability may prove to be the better options since they give a means to accomplish project goals without going over budget.

In addition, the fast changing field of artificial intelligence demands that technologies be chosen with the future in mind. Given the speed at which technology is developing, tools that are useful now may eventually be replaced by more advanced options. Therefore, it may be advantageous to take a visionary approach, in which the selection process is informed by both present needs and future expectations. Tools with the capacity to be integrated with future technologies and scaled up can potentially be more long-lasting, offering a foundation for steady development and expansion.

Moreover, adherence to regulatory standards and ethical considerations are crucial aspects of the choosing process. It is essential to follow data privacy and security standards in an area where data is a critical resource. It can be beneficial to have tools that provide features that make it easier to comply with regulatory standards since they promote an atmosphere in which data processing and management adhere to ethical and legal standards.

In conclusion, choosing the appropriate tools for a task in the intricate field of artificial intelligence is a complex process including many different factors. It is a process that involves several factors, such as the size of the project, the experience of the team, the project's orientation, preferred programming language, hardware infrastructure, community support, financial concerns, and ethical compliance. It's a journey that calls for a keen observation, a thorough comprehension of the workings of the project, and a forward-thinking strategy that looks beyond the present moment to a time when artificial intelligence will be a leading force in innovation and advancement.

It's critical to keep in mind that there is no one-size-fits-all approach to tool selection as we navigate this ever-changing terrain. It's a complex procedure where achieving the ideal balance between several elements might lead to the successful completion of the project. It's an undertaking where the appropriate tools working together with the correct knowledge can open up new possibilities and create an atmosphere that allows AI's revolutionary capacity to be fully realized. We may steer the ship toward a future in which artificial intelligence (AI) serves as a beacon of innovation, accelerating development and bringing in a new era of technological progression marked by intelligence, efficiency, and previously unheard-of capabilities, by carefully considering and making wise choices.

Ensuring computational efficiency

A project's success or failure in the field of AI and ML can be determined by its computational efficiency, which is a fundamental component of these technologies. It is the combination of a variety of approaches, methods, and tactics that combine to maximize the use of computational resources, allowing for quicker processing times, better performance, and the effective application of AI models. The modern era places even more emphasis on computing efficiency as we delve deeper into the realm of big data and sophisticated algorithms. In this section, we will delve into the nuances of computational efficiency and clarify its crucial function within the field of artificial intelligence.

It is wise to start by learning about the theoretical foundations of computing efficiency. It is a theory based on making the best use of all available computational resources, including memory, processing time, and storage capacity. The fundamental idea is to carry out operations in a way that reduces the amount of resources used, which promotes a quick and effective computational process. Numerous strategies, including parallel computing, effective data structures, optimum algorithm choices, and utilizing the capabilities of contemporary hardware designs, can be used to accomplish this.

An essential component in the quest for computer efficiency is algorithm optimization. Artificial intelligence systems are primarily composed of algorithms, which coordinate the series of actions required to convert unprocessed input into meaningful outputs. Algorithm complexity, however, can differ greatly, with some requiring a large number of computer resources. In this case, the Big O notation—a theoretical framework for characterizing an algorithm's computational complexity—can be rather helpful. Large gains in processing performance can be obtained by examining and choosing algorithms with advantageous Big O notation values. Moreover, algorithmic strategies that eliminate unnecessary calculations, including memorization and dynamic programming, can further improve efficiency.

There is still another effective way to attain computational efficiency: parallel computing. Operations are carried out one after the other in traditional sequential computing, which can take a while, especially for complicated jobs. Contrarily, parallel computing makes use of several processing units' capabilities to carry out tasks simultaneously, greatly cutting down on computation time. In the field of ML and DL, where algorithms frequently require a huge number of computations, this approach is especially helpful. It is feasible to significantly reduce processing time and increase computational efficiency by splitting up these operations across several processors.

The part that effective data structures play in guaranteeing computing performance is equally important. A computer system's data structures, which determine how the data is arranged and stored, have a big impact on computing performance. An environment where computational resources are used as efficiently as possible can be fostered by efficient data structures, which are distinguished by minimal memory utilization and quick data retrieval capabilities. In this attempt, methods like data compression—which minimizes the size of data sets—and indexing—which speeds up data retrieval—can be quite helpful. In addition, the deliberate choice of data structures that correspond with the particular needs of an algorithm can also improve efficiency, allowing for quick and effective computations.

As we continue to explore the boundaries of computational efficiency, current hardware architectures play an increasingly important role. A paradigm shift in hardware design has occurred in recent years, with a greater focus on specialized hardware that is optimized for particular tasks. For example, graphics processing units (GPUs) have become invaluable partners in the field of deep learning, providing parallel processing capacity that can greatly speed up calculations. Similarly, another way to improve computational efficiency is to use Tensor Processing Units (TPUs), which are made especially for tensor computations, which are common in deep learning. Significant gains in processing performance can be made by utilizing the capabilities of these specific hardware designs, which will help to create an atmosphere in which AI models can be trained and used effectively.

To further achieve computational efficiency, software framework optimization and selection are essential. Various software frameworks, like as TensorFlow, PyTorch, Keras, and others, are frequently used in modern AI projects. Each framework has its unique characteristics and capabilities. By optimizing these frameworks using methods like kernel fusion and graph optimization, computing performance can be greatly increased. Furthermore, productivity can be further increased by promoting interoperability across various frameworks through programs like the Open Neural Network Exchange (ONNX), which offers a platform for the streamlined and effective development and deployment of AI models.

Computational efficiency is more than just technical; it's a way of thinking that looks ahead, anticipating the direction that technology will go. In an area where progress is made quickly, the quest for computing efficiency is an ever-changing process that calls for creativity and flexibility. Future developments in computing, including quantum computing, present exciting opportunities to reach previously unattainable levels of processing efficiency, expanding the field of artificial intelligence. As a result, maintaining computational efficiency is both a technical and a visionary activity, one in which the limits of what is feasible are always being pushed through invention and discovery.

Furthermore, computational efficiency is important for reasons that go beyond technology and have a big impact on environmental sustainability. In a time when technology's effects on the environment are being closely examined, computational efficiency shows promise as a means of lowering AI activities' carbon footprint. A future in which technology and nature coexist peacefully can be fostered by achieving a healthy balance between technical growth and environmental sustainability through improved algorithms and energy-efficient hardware.

In conclusion, computational efficiency is a critical element in the field of artificial intelligence, representing a combination of tactics, methods, and approaches that collaborate to maximize computational performance. It is feasible to create an environment that is successful, fast, and efficient by utilizing modern hardware designs, parallel processing, optimized algorithms, and efficient data structures. Moreover, computational efficiency is a dynamic and forward-thinking endeavor that opens up new technological frontiers through creativity and innovative methods.

At this point in time, when artificial intelligence is about to enter a new age, the quest of computing efficiency becomes increasingly important. It has the potential to both accelerate the successful implementation of AI systems and promote a sustainable balance between technology and the environment. It is a journey that represents the spirit of creativity, an unwavering quest for excellence, and the desire to realize artificial intelligence's full potential. We may negotiate the challenging terrain of computing efficiency by strategically combining technical expertise with creative thinking, leading the way towards a future marked by intelligence, innovation, and previously unheard-of capabilities.

CHAPTER V

Data: The Fuel for AI

Importance of quality data

High-quality data plays a crucial role in the rapidly changing field of artificial intelligence, providing the foundation for complex machine learning and deep learning algorithms. Accuracy, completeness, and relevance are the hallmarks of quality data, which is the essence of trustworthy information that can support well-informed decision-making. This section delves into the complex web of quality data, examining its significance in a number of areas such as business intelligence, data analytics, machine learning, and its vital role in directing the current global digital revolution. In addition, we will examine the subtleties that define data quality and the significant effects it has on different industries, resulting in a more nuanced knowledge of the necessity of maintaining and promoting high-quality data in the era of artificial intelligence.

Appreciating the fundamental significance that high-quality data plays in machine learning and deep learning paradigms is the first step towards comprehending the critical role that quality data plays. Data is the raw material used in the field of artificial intelligence to power the intricate algorithms and computational procedures that form the foundation of these technologies. In this context, quality data is defined as information that is clear, organized, and free of errors and inconsistencies. This makes it easier to create AI models that are dependable and strong. The ability of data to accurately represent the phenomena it aims to describe is fundamental to quality data as it establishes a strong base for the training and evolution of machine learning algorithms.

Apart from being precise, high-quality data also has various other attributes that greatly increase its worth. It is thorough, making sure that all pertinent facets of the phenomenon are recorded, allowing for a comprehensive examination that can produce subtle revelations. Because it reflects the most recent condition of circumstances, it is timely and allows for meaningful and actionable evaluations and predictions. Furthermore, high-quality data is widely accessible and available in forms that are simple for different analytical tools to consume and analyse, facilitating a smooth information flow that can support thoughtful decision-making processes. It also maintains consistency, with a consistent format and structure that makes data processing and analytics easier.

As we delve more into the nuances of quality data, we see that its importance extends beyond machine learning and deep learning to a wide range of industries and areas. High-quality data is a powerful instrument in business intelligence that can help inform strategic decision-making. Business executives can gain important insights into customer preferences, market trends, and competitive environments through the lens of high-quality data, enabling strategies that are well-researched and supported by data. A deeper comprehension of business dynamics can be facilitated by high-quality data, which gives firms the capacity to improve customer satisfaction, streamline processes, and increase profitability.

Additionally, the importance of high-quality data is highlighted in the context of data analytics, an area in which data is broken down and examined in order to glean insightful information. Analyses that are both in-depth and perceptive are made possible by quality data, which is distinguished by its precision and completeness. High-quality data may be converted into useful insights using advanced analytical approaches, giving businesses a road map to successfully negotiate the challenging terrain of the contemporary business environment. Furthermore, high-quality data may support predictive analytics, which helps businesses foresee trends and dynamics in the future. This allows them to develop proactive plans that can reduce risks and take advantage of opportunities.

Furthermore, high-quality data is essential to scientific study since it makes studies more trustworthy and rigorous. Data is the foundation of empirical investigations in the field of research; it provides the evidence that theories and hypotheses are based upon. In this sense, quality data represents information that is legitimate and trustworthy, offering a solid platform for doing scientific research. Researchers can explore the complexities of different phenomena in great detail through the prism of high-quality data, developing a comprehensive understanding that can further knowledge in a variety of domains.

Further investigation reveals that the digital age has made data-driven decision-making the standard rather than the exception, emphasizing the value of high-quality data. Being able to separate the wheat from the chaff in a world full with data becomes an essential skill. In a sea of data that is frequently colored by noise and mistakes, quality data acts as a beacon of dependability, offering a source of information that can be depended upon. A clear and accurate depiction of phenomena is another way that high-quality data promotes transparency, which can help with decision-making and build stakeholder trust.

On a larger scale, quality data has a function in societal domains, impacting governance and policy formation. When quality data is in the hands of policymakers, it may be a powerful instrument for creating policies that are both efficient and sensitive to the demands of the public. Governments may more precisely and effectively handle complex societal concerns by using data-driven policy making. Moreover, high-quality data can support participatory government, which promotes an environment of accountability and transparency where choices are supported by facts and evidence rather than theories and guesswork.

Furthermore, the fundamentals of high-quality data have a significant impact on innovation and the development of new technologies. Technologists and innovators rely largely on high-quality data to support their work, using the insights it provides to create new and powerful solutions. High-quality data is a powerful tool for innovation in the rapidly evolving field of technology, enabling breakthroughs that have the potential to completely transform entire sectors and paradigms. The limits of what is conceivable are constantly being pushed through the prism of high-quality data, opening the door for a future full of technical wonders and previously unheard-of possibilities.

However, there are obstacles in the way of promoting high-quality data. The necessity of data governance and management has become more apparent due to the multiplicity of data sources and the growing intricacy of data environments. Institutions and organizations are realizing more and more how important it is to set up strong data governance frameworks that can guarantee data quality across the whole data lifecycle. A concentrated effort is needed to develop and preserve data quality, from data collection to data processing and analysis, creating an atmosphere where data may function as a trustworthy and useful resource.

Moreover, the pursuit of high-quality data demands a cooperative strategy, in which several stakeholders cooperate to advance the shared objective of improving data quality. A deliberate effort is needed to foster a culture of data quality, where the value of high-quality data is acknowledged and nurtured, involving everyone from data scientists and analysts to company executives and legislators. Furthermore, training and education are essential for promoting data literacy because they give people the abilities to recognize high-quality data and use it wisely in a variety of situations.

As we move closer to the end of this discussion, it becomes clear that high-quality data is at the intersection of business, technology, and society. It is a crucial factor that can promote growth and advancement. The value of high-quality data is especially relevant in the digital age, as data is now a valuable resource that can impact many aspects of human life. The function of quality data is extensive and pervasive, ranging from propelling technical developments to promoting informed decision-making in enterprises and governance.

In conclusion, it is impossible to exaggerate the importance of high-quality data in today's environment. It acts as the foundation for the artificial intelligence edifice, promoting innovations that are revolutionary and game-changing. Developing high-quality data is an ongoing process that requires attention to detail, perseverance, and a dedication to quality. The need to cultivate high-quality data is becoming more and more urgent as we approach a future reliant on data; we are being called to embrace the subtleties of data quality and create a setting in which it can grow and prosper. By means of a coordinated endeavor involving education, cooperation, and creativity, we may cultivate a future in which high-quality data functions as a dependable lighthouse, propelling advancement and cultivating a world marked by intelligence, comprehension, and unparalleled potential.

Data preprocessing and cleaning

Preprocessing and cleaning data are the cornerstones of creating artificial intelligence systems that are both intelligent and resilient. These preliminary actions are crucial to guaranteeing that the unprocessed data, which frequently has many anomalies and inconsistencies, is converted into a format that is dependable and consistent, which makes it easier to create AI models that are correct and effective. We explore the complexities of data preprocessing and cleaning in detail in this section, identifying the many facets involved and their vital function in the data pipeline.

Data preprocessing and cleaning become essential processes in the complex realm of data science and artificial intelligence, laying the groundwork for the latter stages of data analysis and model building. In essence, data preparation is the act of converting unprocessed data into a format better suited for analysis; this process frequently entails a number of processes, such as data reduction, data transformation, and data cleaning. Data cleaning, on the other hand, is a subset of data preprocessing that focuses on finding and fixing mistakes and inconsistencies in the data to improve its quality. Preprocessing and cleaning data go hand in hand to create the conditions for an efficient and smooth data analysis process.

During the first stages of data preprocessing, data cleaning is usually the main focus. Data cleaning is a procedure that requires extreme attention to detail and a never-ending quest for correctness. Numerous responsibilities, including finding and managing missing values, reducing noise in the data, identifying and eliminating outliers, and resolving conflicts, are part of data cleaning. Ensuring that the data is of excellent quality and free from errors and discrepancies is crucial since they may affect the accuracy of the analytical models that are produced later. Data cleaning is a science and an art process that calls for a thorough comprehension of the data as well as the use of a variety of tools and approaches to find and fix problems.

One essential component of data cleaning is handling missing values. A number of factors, including irregularities in data gathering procedures, omissions, and mistakes in data entry, might result in missing results. The trustworthiness of the results can be jeopardized by the introduction of biases and mistakes in the data analysis caused by missing values. Missing values can be handled using a variety of techniques, such as data deletion, which removes all occurrences of missing values from the dataset, or data imputation, which replaces missing values with estimates based on other available data. The type of data and the degree of missing values frequently influence the method selection, necessitating a sophisticated approach that takes the analysis's possible effects into account.

Smoothing noisy data is also included in the data preprocessing task. Random errors or changes in the data that can mask underlying patterns and correlations are referred to as noisy data. Smoothing is the process of reducing noise in data to improve clarity and enable more accurate analysis. Various approaches, including binning, regression, or clustering, are applied. Preserving the fundamental features of the data while removing random fluctuations that can impede analysis is the aim of smoothing.

Data preprocessing includes handling missing values, smoothing noisy data, and identifying and eliminating outliers. Data points known as outliers are those that substantially depart from the general pattern; these abnormalities, errors, or special situations are frequently the cause of outliers. Outliers have the potential to distort analysis results and produce false conclusions. To find outliers, a variety of statistical techniques can be used, such as box and scatter plots and statistical tests like the Z-score and IQR method. Once located, outliers can be fixed or eliminated, improving the data's dependability.

Another essential component of data preprocessing is data transformation, which aims to change data into a format better suited for analysis. Data transformation can include a number of different operations, like standardization, which rescales data values to have a mean of zero and a standard deviation of one, or normalization, which scales data values to fall within a given range. Furthermore, in order to capture particular traits or relationships, data transformation may entail the generation of derived variables, which are new variables based on preexisting ones. The process of data transformation involves reshaping and restructuring the data to enable a more efficient and perceptive examination.

A technique used in data preparation to lower the amount of data without sacrificing its important qualities is called data reduction. The analysis of large datasets can be time-consuming and computationally demanding. Data can be made more manageable and easier to examine by using data reduction techniques including dimensionality reduction, binning, histograms, and clustering. By reducing the complexity of the data, data reduction makes it possible to analyze the data more quickly and effectively without sacrificing the quality of the insights gained.

As we continue, it becomes clear that data cleaning and preprocessing are essential parts of the bigger data pipeline rather than stand-alone procedures. These procedures have an impact on the quality and reliability of the outcomes and are intimately related to later stages like data analysis and model creation. As a result, it is essential to approach data preprocessing and cleaning from a holistic standpoint, comprehending how it relates to other phases of the data pipeline and how crucial it is to the project's success as a whole.

Furthermore, in the context of machine learning and artificial intelligence, the significance of data preprocessing and cleaning cannot be emphasized. The performance of the created models in these sectors is contingent upon the quality of the data. Trains machine learning models that are robust and dependable require high-quality data that is complete, accurate, and consistent. The data is improved and refined through rigorous data preprocessing and cleaning, giving advanced AI algorithms a strong base on which to operate.

Additionally, the preprocessing and cleaning of data necessitates a thorough comprehension of the available data, which calls for a cooperative approach involving multiple stakeholders. To specify the standards for data quality, locate probable sources of mistakes, and create plans to fix them, data scientists, domain experts, and business executives must collaborate. The process can also be facilitated by the use of cutting-edge tools and technology, which make it possible to automate some jobs and increase the process' efficacy and efficiency.

As we approach the end of this discussion, it will become clear that data cleaning and preprocessing are important procedures that affect the success of data-driven projects rather than being merely technicalities. The efforts to harness the power of data to drive insights and innovations are supported by these procedures, which exemplify the values of thoroughness, precision, and quality. We prepare the way for a data-driven future marked by intelligence, insight, and an unwavering commitment to quality through rigorous data preprocessing and cleaning.

Ultimately, data preprocessing and cleaning are the defenders of data quality, making sure that the data that forms the foundation of artificial intelligence systems is robust and dependable. The significance of these procedures increases as we delve deeper into the fields of data science and artificial intelligence, necessitating a fresh emphasis on improving data quality through careful preprocessing and cleaning. We can create a data environment that is rich and dependable by combining knowledge, cooperation, and creativity. This will open the door for the development of clean, high-quality data that will power artificial intelligence systems in the future.

Techniques for data augmentation

The importance of data is paramount in the rapidly developing field of artificial intelligence, as it provides the foundation for the development of complex models and algorithms. While a sizable amount of data is necessary, data augmentation techniques can improve the diversity and richness of the data by adding another layer of complexity to the training datasets, which enhances the overall performance of machine learning and deep learning models. This section examines several data augmentation methods, their ramifications, and the many advantages they provide for building artificial intelligence systems.

In the introductory discussion of data augmentation, it is important to emphasize the basic function it performs within the framework of deep learning and machine learning. The approach of data augmentation is employed to enhance the quantity and variety of training data while avoiding the need for new data collection. The aforementioned procedure entails implementing diverse modifications to the current dataset, thereby producing novel instances that preserve the fundamental attributes of the initial data. Data augmentation increases the model's ability to generalize and adjust to previously unseen data, which lowers the risk of overfitting and promotes a more stable and dependable model.

Investigating data augmentation methods needs a holistic strategy, with specific attention devoted to different categories of data, such as text, audio, and image data, each of which has unique properties and calls for a different kind of augmentation.

In the field of image data augmentation, there are many different strategies available that provide a multitude of ways to produce new and varied instances by transforming and modifying the existing photos. Geometric transformations, which include flipping, rotating, and cropping, are among the fundamental methods used in the augmentation of image data. Rotation introduces a change in perspective by rotating the image by a specific angle. Flipping is another simple yet powerful method that creates a distinct perspective of the same object by mirroring the image either vertically or horizontally. Cropping, on the other hand, concentrates on taking out particular areas of the picture to highlight certain aspects and possibly eliminate others.

Moreover, within the realm of image data augmentation, a multitude of pixel-level adjustments are available to change the color, texture, and lighting of the photos. The lighting of the image can be altered using techniques like brightness and contrast alteration to create variations that resemble various environmental circumstances. Comparably, color jittering produces changes that mimic various lighting situations and camera settings by adjusting the image's color balance. Additionally, methods such as noise injection add a degree of randomization to the pixel values, producing data that is more resistant to noise and changes found in the actual world.

Moving forward, we come across the interesting area of text data augmentation, which is evidence of the creativity and inventiveness in data science. Text data augmentation provides a multitude of approaches that enrich the text data manifold, although being somewhat more sophisticated than image data augmentation. Synonym replacement is a core technique in text data augmentation, where words in the text are swapped out for their synonyms, adding lexical diversity while maintaining semantic content. Back translation is an additional technique that entails translating a document to another language and then back to the original. This process frequently yields somewhat altered wording while maintaining the main idea. Sentence rearranging and random word insertion, deletion, and swapping are examples of techniques that generate text structural variations and promote a rich and diverse dataset.

As we investigate further, we enter the field of audio data augmentation, which offers a special set of possibilities and difficulties. Due to the temporal and spectral dimensions of audio data, specific techniques are needed to manipulate these aspects in order to produce new and varied instances. Variations that simulate various acoustic environments and conditions are introduced through techniques like time stretching, which modifies the audio's speed without changing its pitch, and pitch shifting, which modifies the audio's pitch without changing its speed. Furthermore, incorporating background noise or using filters to change the audio's frequency characteristics help to build a more resilient and varied dataset that can handle the noise and changes found in real-world situations.

Beyond the technical terms, it is imperative to consider the wider ramifications of data augmentation in the context of artificial intelligence. In addition to being a method for boosting the dataset's diversity and richness, data augmentation represents a philosophical perspective on comprehending and portraying the intricate, multidimensional character of the real world. By means of data augmentation, our goal is to develop artificial intelligence systems that are not only highly skilled in their technical aspects but also have a more profound comprehension of the subtleties and differences that exist in the actual world. Data augmentation proves to be a potent ally in this attempt, promoting more resilient, intelligent, and adaptive models.

Moreover, the incorporation of data augmentation methodologies into the data pipeline demands a deliberate approach that considers multiple elements, including the type of data, the particular demands of the task, and the possible influence on the model's efficacy. Instead of being a random choice, the data augmentation strategies are chosen strategically to improve the model's capacity to generalize and adjust to new, unobserved input. Data augmentation can be a highly effective tool in the creation of artificial intelligence systems, increasing their success and effectiveness with careful planning and implementation.

Furthermore, the developments in the field of data augmentation are indicative of the more general tendencies in artificial intelligence, which are defined by creativity, research, and an unwavering quest for perfection. Research and experimentation have led to the creation of new, sophisticated data augmentation techniques that push the boundaries of what is possible and promote a dynamic, ever-evolving field. By working together and exchanging ideas, the community aims to strengthen the foundations already in place and develop methods that are more dependable and efficient while also advancing the development of powerful artificial intelligence systems.

As this discussion draws to a close, it is necessary to emphasize the critical role that data augmentation plays in the artificial intelligence landscape. By using data augmentation, we hope to create models that can navigate the subtleties and complexities that are characteristic of real-world scenarios by bridging the gap between the small, restricted datasets and the vast, varied actual world. We hope to leverage the power of data augmentation in promoting the development of a new generation of intelligent and complex artificial intelligence systems through a concentrated effort that includes research, innovation, and application.

In conclusion, data augmentation represents a ray of hope and advancement in the realm of artificial intelligence, contributing to the improvement of training datasets' quality and diversity, which in turn produces more resilient and dependable models. The importance of data augmentation grows as we explore the domains of machine learning and deep learning. It provides a means of overcoming data constraints and striving to develop models that accurately capture the dynamic, complex nature of the real world. We set out on a quest of exploration and discovery through data augmentation, hoping to unlock the mysteries of data and use its potential to power a future full of intelligence, insight, and previously unimaginable capabilities.

CHAPTER VI

Training and Optimization

The process of training an AI model

The phrase artificial intelligence (AI) is almost synonymous for innovation and advancement in the modern day. Due to its intricate networks and algorithms, artificial intelligence (AI) is transforming many sectors and enabling things that were previously unthinkable. The complex process of training AI models, which includes a number of processes and phases that are all essential to creating an intelligent system, is at the heart of AI's power. This section aims to clarify this procedure, outlining each step and revealing the complexities associated with teaching an AI model.

The process of training an AI model begins with the identification of a task or problem that the model is intended to accomplish or resolve. This first stage is very important since it establishes the foundation for the next stages. It demands that the job at hand be thoroughly analyzed and understood, that the objectives be precisely defined, and that a clear path be established for the project to follow. Collaboration between domain experts and also data scientists is common during this stage in order to identify precise requirements and any obstacles that may occur throughout the model's development.

After the issue has been recognized and clearly stated, gathering data is a crucial next step in the procedure. Data is without a doubt the foundation around which the entire AI model is constructed. The final model's performance is directly impacted by the type and volume of data. Data may originate from a number of sources, such as corporate databases, open-source datasets, or information obtained by web scraping. The type of data used to train the model could include text, graphics, or numerical values, depending on the nature of the problem. Each type of data has its own unique set of properties.

After the acquisition of data, data preprocessing becomes an essential part of the training process. In this stage, the data must be cleaned, any missing or inconsistent data must be handled, and the data may need to be formatted such that it can easily used for model training. In order to make it easier to assess the model's performance later on, it may also involve splitting the data into training, validation, and testing sets. This phase also includes feature extraction and selection, where pertinent characteristics are found and chosen according to how they might affect the prediction power of the model.

The journey continues by choosing a suitable model or algorithm once a clear and well-prepared dataset is at hand. The type of data, the difficulty of the problem, and the available computer resources are some of the variables that influence the model choice. This stage frequently entails trying out different models, each with its own distinct set of parameters and features, to see which one performs the best for the task at hand. Simpler models, like linear regression for predictive analytics, can be used to tackle more complicated problems like picture or speech recognition, which call for deep learning models.

We reach the phase of model training as we proceed further along the process, which is frequently regarded as the center of the whole thing. Using the training dataset, the chosen model is trained in this step to learn how to recognize patterns and correlations in the data. To reduce the difference between its predictions and the actual values in the training data, the model modifies its internal parameters, frequently using techniques like gradient descent. This stage involves a lot of calculation and could call for a significant amount of computing power, particularly for complicated models with lots of parameters.

We move from the training phase to the validation and assessment phase. This stage is critical for determining the model's capacity for generalization, or, to put it another way, how well it works with unknown data. To avoid overfitting—a situation in which the model learns the noise in the training data and is unable to generalize well to new data—the validation set, a portion of the data that was not utilized during training, is used to fine-tune the model parameters. After validation, the model is tested on a test set, and depending on the type of problem being handled, its performance is measured using different metrics like accuracy, precision, and recall.

After the evaluation process is completed satisfactorily, the model is deployed, meaning that it can either be incorporated into current systems or made available to end users to carry out the task for which it was trained. This stage could include creating user interfaces, integrating the model into pre-existing software frameworks, or building up APIs for model access. The adventure doesn't exactly finish here, though. The model goes into a phase of ongoing maintenance and monitoring after deployment. Because the real world is dynamic, the model may come with data that differs greatly from the training set. Consequently, ongoing observation makes it possible to promptly update and modify the model in order to guarantee its continued functionality.

We should explore the ethical issues surrounding AI model training in order to have a deeper understanding of the overall picture. The creation and application of AI models has significant social ramifications that impact people on an individual and a community level. Throughout the development process, it is imperative to take into account crucial elements such as data protection, permission, and potential biases in AI models. Fairness, inclusion, and transparency are essential to responsible AI development because they guarantee that the models respect people's rights and privacy and do not reinforce preexisting biases.

Let's face it: building an AI model is a laborious and intricate process, likened to a carefully planned symphony in which every action adds a crucial note to the overall harmonious melody of artificial intelligence. From the first idea to the meticulous data preparation, the rigorous training, and the model's fine-tuning, every stage has its importance and results in a model with the power to transform industries and promote advancement.

A well-thought-out and organized training process is becoming increasingly important as artificial intelligence (AI) continues to advance and carve out niches in a variety of industries, including healthcare, banking, and entertainment. The quest for artificial intelligence is not only a technological undertaking but also a cooperative journey in which multidisciplinary teams collaborate and combine knowledge from diverse fields to create models that are strong, ethical, and responsible.

Additionally, because the industry is dynamic, training AI models must take an adaptive approach that prioritizes ongoing learning and development. More complex and powerful AI models are possible due to the quick development of technology, the growth of processing capacity, and the creation of new approaches and algorithms. Therefore, the process of training an AI model is dynamic and ever-changing, altering as society and technology change over time.

In conclusion, training an AI model is a huge undertaking that encompasses a philosophical and technical journey.

It's a journey where data and algorithms meet science and art to develop intelligent systems that have the power to push the envelope of what is thought to be possible. The emphasis on a systematic and deliberate training process becomes a beacon of progress as we approach a future where artificial intelligence (AI) not only enhances human capabilities but also promotes a more informed, effective, and inclusive society. This is all happening at the dawn of a new era of artificial intelligence. By means of a profound comprehension and admiration of the process involved in training artificial intelligence models, we advance, moving toward a future full of opportunities driven by the might of artificial intelligence.

Cost functions and loss optimization

The field of artificial intelligence is intricate, and the study of cost functions and loss optimization is fundamental to the effectiveness and accuracy of AI models. These mathematical formulas guide the learning trajectory of AI systems, directing them towards accuracy and optimization, much like a compass guides a ship through turbulent seas. In order to better understand cost functions and loss optimization, this section will examine them in detail and show how important a part they have played in the development of artificial intelligence.

To begin with, it is critical to understand what cost functions and loss functions mean in the context of AI and ML. A cost function, sometimes referred to as a loss function, is essentially a mathematical formula that calculates the discrepancy between the model's actual and predicted outputs. This function's main goal is to determine the optimal set of parameters that minimizes this difference, which will help the model become more accurate and have more generalization abilities. The function searches through a number of factors in this frequently intricate, multidimensional space in order to identify the ideal point that represents the lowest cost.

More precisely, depending on the kind of problem being solved, loss functions can be divided into several kinds. When attempting to forecast a continuous value in regression issues, the mean squared error, or MSE, is frequently employed. In order to determine the degree of prediction error, this function computes the square of the difference between the actual and predicted values. On the other hand, the cross-entropy loss function is frequently used for classification issues, where the goal is to divide the data into various groups. In order to maximize the log-likelihood of the correct class label, this function calculates the logarithm of the probabilities given to the true class.

It becomes clear as we continue exploring this mathematical terrain that optimizing the loss function is a crucial phase in the training of AI models. In this sense, optimization algorithms act as navigators, pointing the function in the direction of the ideal location within the parameter space. In the field of artificial intelligence, gradient descent and its variants—such as mini-batch gradient descent and stochastic gradient descent—are frequently used optimization methods. The ultimate objective of these algorithms is to locate the minimal point that represents the lowest cost by iteratively adjusting the model parameters and traveling in the direction of the cost function's sharpest decline.

The idea of loss optimization is more comprehensive than only using mathematical procedures. It includes a comprehensive strategy that takes into account a number of factors, such as model complexity, data quality, and computational efficiency. This is where regularization and other related ideas become useful, giving the optimization process an additional level of complexity. L1 and L2 regularization are two regularization techniques that discourage complex models from overfitting to the training data by introducing a penalty term into the cost function. This mitigates the bias-variance tradeoff that is intrinsic to machine learning models by ensuring that the model not only minimizes the loss but also performs well in terms of generalization to new information.

Going forward, it is important to recognize the complex relationship that exists between cost functions and the general architecture of neural networks, particularly in the context of deep learning. In this domain, the layers of neurons are guided towards an ideal configuration by the cost function, which functions as a compass to precisely capture the underlying patterns in the data. A key element of deep learning is the backpropagation algorithm, which uses the gradients of the cost function to modify the neural network's weights. By propagating the error backwards through the layers, the network can be tuned iteratively to improve performance. The core of deep learning is this complex dance between the neural network and the cost function, which produces models with high-level abstractions and complex representations.

In addition, the field of loss optimization and cost functions is not a static one. The optimization process is being improved by researchers as they continuously explore new routes and strategies in this dynamic and ever-evolving subject. More complex optimization algorithms, including Adam and RMSProp, have recently been developed. These algorithms include adaptive learning rates, enabling quicker and more effective convergence to the optimal point. Furthermore, the optimization process now has an additional dimension due to the development of ideas like batch normalization and dropout techniques, which allow for the creation of deeper and more complicated models without running the risk of overfitting and gradient vanishing.

It is impossible to ignore the computational components of loss optimization in parallel. Because the optimization process involves a lot of computation, it requires a lot of power and resources. The area has undergone a revolution with the introduction of graphics processing units (GPUs) and tensor processing units (TPUs), which offer the computational power needed to navigate the intricate, multi-dimensional space of cost functions, particularly in the deep learning domain. AI capabilities have entered a new era as a result of these advancements, which have made it possible to train bigger and more complicated models.

It is crucial to consider the ethical and responsible application of AI models as we move into the last part of this investigation. The pursuit of minimizing loss and optimizing performance may lead to the development of models that exhibit bias or discrimination. Because it is a mathematical representation, the cost function is unaware of the predictions' social and ethical ramifications. Fairness and ethics must therefore be incorporated into the optimization process in order to guarantee that the models do not reinforce preexisting biases or injustices. This requires a multidisciplinary approach that guides the optimization process with ethical considerations in addition to mathematical concepts, resulting in the construction of AI models that are just and accurate.

With artificial intelligence poised to shape our future, cost functions and loss optimization will play an increasingly important role. These mathematical expressions serve as the foundation of artificial intelligence systems, directing them through a maze of intricacies in the direction of accuracy and precision. The complexity and subtlety of these functions increase with the field's evolution, resulting in models with previously unheard-of capabilities. To ensure that the larger objective of promoting an inclusive and equal society is not eclipsed by the quest of accuracy, it is imperative to proceed cautiously and responsibly along this path towards optimization and efficiency.

In conclusion, the field of cost functions and loss optimization is a lively, dynamic environment that is brimming with subtleties and complexities. This field unites theory and practice with mathematics and computation to produce AI models that have the power to completely transform industries and push the envelope of what is possible. The emphasis on a thorough understanding of cost functions and loss optimization becomes a light of progress as we go forward into this exciting future, leading us towards a time where AI preserves the values of justice and equity while also augmenting human talents. We go forward into a future where artificial intelligence acts as a catalyst for positive change, pushing society towards a horizon full of opportunities and potentialities, with a deep appreciation of the mathematical subtleties and a dedication to ethical AI development.

Overfitting and techniques to prevent it

One phenomenon in particular stands out as particularly difficult in the complex ecosystem of machine learning and artificial intelligence, frequently acting as a barrier to the development of highly efficient, generalized models: overfitting. Overfitting is similar to a story that is too tightly wound around the narrating elements, losing sight of the larger narrative universe and becoming uninteresting in new settings. This basically describes a scenario in which a model learns the noise in the data rather than the underlying pattern, performing incredibly well on training data but horribly on unseen data. This section explores the aspects of overfitting, the consequences it causes, and a variety of methods that can be applied to mitigate this widespread problem in machine learning.

To counteract overfitting, it is important to understand its fundamentals. When a model has too many parameters and is overly complicated, it can match the training set's individual data points too closely, a phenomenon known as overfitting in mathematics. Because it is too adapted to the peculiarities of the training set, the model in this instance struggles to generalize well to new data. It is comparable, in real life terms, to learning the answers to a sequence of questions by heart without comprehending the underlying ideas, which makes it impossible to respond to questions that are repeated in a different setting or format.

Moreover, overfitting has a number of consequences that go beyond the performance indicators. It suggests that the model's predictions on fresh data are unreliable since it hasn't discovered the real underlying patterns in the data. This not only hinders the model's performance but also defeats the goal of machine learning, which is to create models with good generalization to unknown data, providing predictions and insights that are representative of the wider distribution of data.

When one sets out to avoid overfitting, they come across a number of methods that are powerful weapons in their arsenal against this widespread problem. As a first line of defense, data augmentation is frequently used. This entails using different transformations, including flips, rotations, and translations, to create fresh training samples, hence boosting the volume and variety of training data. The model is exposed to a broader array of data points when the data is augmented, which helps to prevent overfitting by forcing the model to learn more generalized features rather than tailoring to the details of the initial training set.

When used with data augmentation, cross-validation is a powerful method for preventing overfitting. Partitioning the training data into 'k' subsets and iteratively training the model on 'k-1' subsets while verifying it on the remaining subset is known as cross-validation, specifically k-fold cross-validation. Every subset serves as the validation set once during the 'k' iterations of this process. This helps spot overfitting early in the training phase and provides a more reliable assessment of the model's performance on unknown data.

Beyond cross-validation and data augmentation, regularization is a guard against overfitting. Regularization methods, like L1 and L2 regularization, penalize model complexity, deterring the development of excessively complicated models that are prone to overfitting. While L2 regularization adds the weights' square to the loss function to promote lower weights, L1 regularization adds the weights' absolute value to the loss function to promote sparsity in the model parameters. These methods support the development of simpler, more broadly applicable models by controlling the complexity of the model.

Another line of defense against overfitting is provided by pruning and early stopping. Pruning is the process of removing nonessential neurons or connections from a neural network in order to reduce model complexity and avoid overfitting. On the other side, early stopping means terminating the training procedure before the model overfits. This is usually done using a validation set, where training is stopped as soon as the validation set's performance begins to decline. By doing this, the model's capacity to generalize effectively to new data is preserved and it is kept from being overly tailored to the training set.

Delving further, one comes across the idea of dropout, a deep learning technique that is frequently used to stop overfitting. During each training cycle, dropout occurs when a portion of the network's neurons are arbitrarily set to zero, hence "dropping out" those neurons. Because it cannot rely on a single neuron to be present throughout training, this encourages the network to acquire redundant representations. Instead of tuning to particular neurons or connections, the network learns to make predictions based on a wider collection of features, which promotes a more robust and generic model.

Furthermore, avoiding overfitting is greatly influenced by the model's design and complexity choices. Choosing large, parameter-rich models is frequently alluring in the hopes that they would capture the nuanced patterns found in the data. But, as a result of the model becoming overtuned to the training set, overfitting may result. Therefore, it is crucial to select a model complexity that matches the intricacy of the issue at hand in order to prevent too complicated models that are prone to overfitting. Furthermore, methods such as model selection and hyperparameter tuning can assist in determining the ideal level of model complexity, resulting in more accurate and broadly applicable models.

As we explore more of this area, it becomes clear that stopping overfitting is a team effort that calls for a variety of methods and approaches rather than a single task. Furthermore, the effort to avoid overfitting penetrates all aspects of the process, not only the training phase but also feature selection, data gathering, and model assessment. It necessitates a thorough strategy that takes into account many aspects of the machine learning process, resulting in models that are robust, accurate, and able to make correct predictions on data that hasn't been seen yet.

Furthermore, avoiding overfitting in the context of artificial intelligence is an ongoing, changing process. Techniques to avoid overfitting must change and adapt as

AI models get more intricate and sophisticated. This field of study is dynamic, with new approaches and techniques being created on a regular basis to address the problems caused by overfitting. This highlights how important it is to have a thorough understanding of the guiding principles and to be dedicated to lifelong learning and adaptation in order to support the creation of AI models that are strong and trustworthy.

In conclusion, overfitting is an important challenge in the development of highly efficient, generalized AI models. This behavior poses a danger to the fundamental goal of machine learning, which is to create models with strong generalization to new and unobserved data. Nevertheless, overfitting may be controlled with a strong toolkit of methods and approaches, leading to more accurate and broadly applicable models. By employing a broad strategy that includes data augmentation, cross-validation, regularization, and other methods, we are moving toward a future in which AI models serve as dependable and efficient lights, able to revolutionize industries and usher in a new age of innovation and development for society. Thus, the battle against overfitting becomes crucial as we stand on the edge of an AI revolution, influencing the course of AI development and deciding how AI will affect society in the future.

Transfer learning and pre-trained models

Transfer learning and pre-trained models have become essential components in the ever-evolving field of artificial intelligence, seamlessly connecting the realms of machine learning effectiveness and efficiency. This method goes beyond the bounds of conventional machine learning models, providing a way to apply past knowledge and insights to new tasks, therefore saving time and computational resources and promoting a culture of ongoing learning and adaptability. This section aims to shed light on the crucial role that pre-trained models play in the ever-changing field of artificial intelligence by delving deeply into the complexities of transfer learning and their abilities.

When machine learning first started off, models had to be trained from scratch, which required a significant quantity of data and processing power. In the early days, models were trained meticulously on particular tasks and functioned in isolated silos with little ability to apply lessons learned from one task to another. The introduction of transfer learning brought about a paradigm change in this field by enabling the seamless transfer of learnings from one activity to another, improving performance on related tasks and saving time and resources throughout the training process.

Fundamentally, transfer learning is based on the notion that skills acquired in one area of problem-solving can be applied to another. In addition to dismantling the silos that defined machine learning's early stages, this promotes a synergistic approach in which models develop and adapt by drawing on prior knowledge. Transfer learning is essentially the essence of learning, which is defined as the process of gaining knowledge and using it in a variety of circumstances.

Taking a pre-trained model—one that has already been trained on a sizable dataset—and optimizing it for a new task is the usual procedure for putting transfer learning into practice. The neural network's layers are adjusted during this fine-tuning process, with the later, more task-specific layers being changed to fit the new task, while the earlier layers, which have learned the general features, are kept. By using pre-trained models, which have already acquired a wealth of features from sizable datasets, this procedure improves performance on novel tasks while frequently requiring less data and processing power than starting from scratch with a new model's training.

There are many models that serve different domains and tasks in the vast and dynamic world of pre-trained models. These models provide a vast reservoir of information and insights obtained from extended training on huge datasets, and they frequently function as the foundation for the transfer learning process. Pre-trained models, such as ResNet for image recognition and BERT for natural language processing, are powerful symbols in the artificial intelligence field. They represent the potential of transfer learning and form the basis of many machine learning tasks.

Pre-trained models, which represent the body of knowledge and developments in the field of artificial intelligence, are also frequently the result of intensive research and development. These models provide a rich and varied basis for transfer learning since they are trained on enormous datasets that cover a broad variety of features and patterns. These models are trained using a significant amount of computational power and knowledge, resulting in models that are both strong and complex and can improve performance on a variety of tasks.

In this context, it becomes imperative to clarify the numerous advantages that transfer learning and pre-trained models offer. To begin with, they drastically cut down on the amount of time and computer power needed to train models. Fine-tuning pre-trained models for new tasks frequently takes a lot less time than training a model from start because the pre-trained models have already learnt a collection of characteristics and patterns. This not only conserves resources but also helps to create an effective and efficient machine learning culture.

Furthermore, because transfer learning and pre-trained models make use of the knowledge gained from earlier training on huge datasets, they frequently need less data for new tasks. This is especially useful in situations when data is expensive or hard to obtain because it makes it possible to create strong models with little data. Furthermore, pre-trained models offer a comprehensive set of characteristics and insights gained from extensive training on a variety of datasets, so one can get greater performance by utilizing their power.

Furthermore, transfer learning promotes a synergistic approach to machine learning, in which models develop and learn by utilizing information and understanding from diverse tasks. By doing so, the conventional silos are broken down and a culture of cooperation and ongoing learning is promoted, allowing models to develop and change as a result of access to a wealth of information and experience. This improves performance on particular tasks as well as opens the door for the creation of more complicated and nuanced models that can solve intricate, multifaceted issues.

As we delve further into this field, it becomes clear that pre-trained models and transfer learning are not merely instruments but rather concepts that capture the spirit of adaptation and learning. They create an environment that is dynamic and ever-changing, where models are living, breathing creatures that are constantly learning and changing based on a wide range of rich and varied experiences and knowledge. Transfer learning and pre-trained models, in a way, embody the essence of artificial intelligence, a discipline defined by learning, adaptability, and evolution, paving the way for advancement and innovation by harnessing the collective wisdom.

It's important to remember, though, that there are obstacles on this journey. Negative transfer, in which the knowledge transferred from the pre-trained model to the new task does not improve performance but rather impedes it, is one of the main challenges in transfer learning. This usually happens when there is insufficient relationship between the pre-trained model and the new task, which results in the transmission of unrelated or false information. This necessitates carefully weighing how well the previously trained model and the new task mesh, resulting in a smooth and advantageous transfer.

Moreover, the process of optimizing pre-trained models for novel tasks frequently necessitates a careful balancing act in which the model must be appropriately modified to fit the novel goal while preserving the important lessons learned from the previous training. This necessitates proficiency and a sophisticated comprehension of the work at hand as well as the model architecture, resulting in an efficient and successful fine-tuning process.

In conclusion, in the ever changing field of artificial intelligence, transfer learning and pre-trained models are invaluable allies. They promote an environment of effectiveness and efficiency in machine learning procedures by emulating the fundamentals of learning and adaption. We create a route that is resource- and time-efficient by utilizing the power of pre-trained models, which encourages the construction of strong, complex models that can enhance performance on a variety of tasks. As we approach the dawn of a new era in artificial intelligence, pre-trained models and transfer learning present a bright and promising route. They illuminate the path towards an era of ongoing innovation, teamwork, and learning, guiding the field of artificial intelligence towards unprecedented heights of success.

CHAPTER VII

Challenges in AI, ML, and DL

Ethical considerations

With artificial intelligence fields still developing and growing, the field of ethics plays a crucial part in determining how this field will develop in the future. These factors provide as the moral compass that directs the creation, application, and advancement of artificial intelligence technologies. They also support the path towards a future in which AI is a positive force that promotes development and well-being while defending the ideals and standards that form the foundation of our society. Artificial intelligence holds great promise for changing many elements of our society, but it also raises a number of ethical concerns that need to be considered, including privacy, justice, accountability, and the preservation of human dignity. In this section, we go deeply into the maze-like passageways of ethical issues surrounding artificial intelligence, navigating the complex web of moral imperatives, obligations, and challenges that underpin this ever-changing field.

Before we go on this adventure, it is important to emphasize that artificial intelligence—a field defined by the development of machines that can replicate human thought processes and behavior—has the potential to have a substantial impact on a number of areas of human existence. AI has impacted many areas of our society, including healthcare, education, banking, and transportation. It has also brought with it a wealth of potential as well as challenges. Here, the field of ethics becomes an important factor that directs the creation and application of these technologies, creating an environment in which AI functions inside the bounds set by ethics and social norms.

The protection of privacy is one of the main issues in the field of AI ethics. In a time when data is essential to AI systems, careful consideration must be given to how it is gathered, stored, and used in order to preserve people's privacy. The potential for invasive surveillance and data breaches is brought about by AI's growing capacity to analyze and use data, endangering people's security and privacy. Therefore, it is morally required to create and implement AI systems that respect strict data protection guidelines, guaranteeing the privacy and confidentiality of personal information. Furthermore, people ought to be free to manage their own data, encouraging a culture of informed consent in which people are conscious of the uses of their data and empowered to make decisions about its use.

As we proceed, we come across the difficult terrain of prejudice and fairness. Artificial intelligence (AI) systems are prone to acquiring the preconceptions and biases that are prevalent in our culture since they are taught using real-world data. When ingrained in AI systems, these prejudices have the potential to worsen already-existing inequalities and promote discrimination. This makes the fairness principle—which calls for the creation of AI systems devoid of biases that advance equity and justice—an essential ethical consideration. This calls for a concentrated effort to find and remove biases in data and algorithms, creating an environment where AI is used as a tool to advance inclusivity and justice rather than to reinforce discrimination.

Deeper exploration reveals the crucial component of transparency and accountability. Integrating artificial intelligence technologies into several domains of human existence requires a structure that ensures these systems operate transparently and incorporates accountability measures. This is especially relevant when considering AI decision-making systems, which could impact important facets of human existence including work, healthcare, and law enforcement. When AI systems operate transparently, people can comprehend the reasoning behind the decisions these systems make, which in turn builds confidence and trust in the systems. Accountability also guarantees that security measures are in place to stop abuse and hold the systems responsible for any unfavorable results.

We move forward and come across the crucial area of human agency and dignity. In the field of artificial intelligence, where computers are capable of imitating human thought processes and actions, it is imperative to guarantee that the advancement and implementation of these technologies do not compromise human autonomy and dignity. This entails creating an environment in which AI complements human abilities rather than subduings or dominates them. A key ethical consideration is the concept of "human-centered AI," which promotes the creation of AI systems that put human dignity and well-being first. This creates a mutually beneficial relationship between humans and machines in which the latter act as allies in the quest of human flourishing.

Additionally, as we move across this terrain, the area of societal impact becomes more and more important, necessitating an assessment of the wider effects of AI on society. The emergence of AI has the potential to profoundly impact our society's socioeconomic structure, bringing about changes that may affect social relationships, job trends, and economic dynamics. In this regard, it is critical to evaluate the possible social effects of AI and to support a growth path that is in line with the more general objectives of societal advancement and well-being. This calls for a multi-stakeholder strategy in which different actors work together to influence the development and application of AI in a way that promotes favorable societal outcomes. These actors include governments, business, and civil society.

Furthermore, the field of AI ethics invites a thorough reflection on the moral obligations that come along with building intelligent computers. It is our responsibility as the developers and stewards of these technologies to resolve the ethical challenges and obstacles that AI development presents. This entails promoting an ethical culture of accountability and integrity among the AI community and adhering to research and development best practices. In addition, the ethical stewardship of AI necessitates ongoing assessment and modification, whereby we respond to newly arising problems and ethical issues, cultivating a dynamic, changing ethical environment that adjusts to the shifting boundaries of the AI domain.

Now that we have come to the conclusion of this journey, it is important to emphasize that the field of ethical issues in AI is dynamic and ever-changing, marked by ongoing discussion, reflection, and adaptation. It invites collaboration amongst many stakeholders in order to mold AI's ethical course and create a future in which the technology advances society and improves human welfare.

In conclusion, the field of ethical considerations in artificial intelligence is a dynamic and diverse area that covers a wide range of concerns, such as privacy, justice, accountability, human dignity, and the influence on society. We see that the journey through the intricate and winding labyrinths of AI ethics is marked by constant investigation, discussion, and modification, paving the way for a time when AI functions within the bounds set by moral standards and cultural norms. By working together to tackle the plethora of ethical problems and conundrums, we pave the way for a time when artificial intelligence (AI) will be a positive force in the world, improving people's quality of life and promoting fairness, equality, and wellbeing. It is our obligation as stewards of this changing environment to responsibly and ethically negotiate the ethical complexities, guiding the development of artificial intelligence in a way that protects the values and ideals that are fundamental to what it is to be human.

Bias and fairness in AI

As we enter a new era of rapid technological progress, with artificial intelligence (AI) permeating many aspects of daily life, the consequences of bias and the need to ensure fairness have become important topics of discussion. Due to AI's significant impact on a wide range of industries, including healthcare, banking, justice, and employment, it is even more critical than ever to eliminate bias and promote fairness in AI systems. Comprehending this requirement invites a detailed investigation into the multifaceted domains in which bias appears and the tactics that might be developed to promote equity in the AI ecosystem. We will explore the depths of bias and fairness in artificial intelligence in this section, removing the layers that make up this important area of ethics in AI.

It is essential to shed light on the nature of bias in AI systems in order to start this conversation. In essence, bias is a departure from objectivity, and it can enter AI systems in a number of ways. It is primarily embedded in the data that these algorithms are trained with. Any underlying biases in the data may be absorbed by the AI system because AI models learn and adjust based on the information provided to them. Furthermore, bias may originate from the predispositions of the developers who created these systems, and these predispositions may be reflected in the algorithms that control how these systems function. Because of this, AI systems may unintentionally turn into instruments that reinforce and magnify societal inequalities and biases. Therefore, recognizing and comprehending these biases is the first step in promoting fairness in the field of artificial intelligence.

One of the crucial domains where bias is evidently displayed is algorithmic decision-making across multiple industries, particularly in the fields of law enforcement, loan approvals, and recruitment. For example, based on the data it was trained on, AI systems intended to screen job candidates may favor certain demographics over others. Similar to this, racial or ethnic biases in AI systems may impact the impartiality and fairness of law enforcement procedures. As a result, these biases have the potential to undermine the concepts of justice and fairness by resulting in the continuation of discrimination and inequality. As such, assessing the consequences of these biases and developing mitigation techniques becomes imperative in the modern AI environment.

In order to promote fairness in AI, a multimodal strategy incorporating several processes and tactics is necessary. To begin with, this calls for a close examination of the data that was utilized to train these programs. Preserving the representativeness and diversity of data is a crucial first step towards eliminating bias. We can create AI systems that are more unbiased and fair by combining a wide range of data that captures different viewpoints and experiences. Moreover, promoting openness in the way AI systems operate can greatly facilitate the improvement of fairness. We enable an objective assessment of these systems and the discovery and rectification of any biases that may be ingrained in them by making the algorithms transparent.

In addition, it is important to recognize that interdisciplinary cooperation promotes fairness. Insights from sociology, psychology, ethics, and other fields can enhance our comprehension of the many subtleties of bias and facilitate the development of tactics that promote fairness. Furthermore, involving a variety of people in the creation and assessment of AI systems can be a powerful strategy for overcoming biases. This entails encouraging diversity among the development teams for these systems, bringing in a wide range of viewpoints and experiences that can help create AI systems that are more fair and balanced.

Fairness also requires the AI community to cultivate an ethical culture, which is a crucial component. This entails developing an attitude that places a high value on moral issues, such as justice, and makes them key considerations for developing AI systems. The AI community can benefit greatly from training courses and workshops that explain the subtleties of bias and methods for reducing it. These can help to create an ethical culture. Furthermore, ethical frameworks and rules can act as compass points, pointing the community in the direction of creating AI systems that respect equity and fairness.

When we delve deeper into this field's complexities, algorithmic fairness becomes an essential focus. It becomes imperative to create algorithms that intentionally avoid discriminating against particular groups and are fair in their design. In order to do this, fairness restrictions must be incorporated into the algorithms, directing them to produce more equal and balanced results. Furthermore, investigating cutting-edge approaches such as fairness-enhancing interventions— which try to rectify biases in data and algorithms— remains a potential path for promoting fairness in artificial intelligence.

However, there are many obstacles and complexity in the way of achieving fairness. It is a difficult undertaking to strike a balance between the goals of fairness and other operational goals like accuracy and efficiency. Furthermore, because fairness encompasses a wide range of viewpoints and aspects, precisely defining it can be a challenging task. Therefore, developing a conversation that involves a range of stakeholders—including academics, corporate executives, policymakers, and members of civil society—becomes crucial to developing a thorough strategy for ensuring fairness in AI.

Furthermore, laws and regulatory frameworks that control the creation and application of AI systems show up as essential tools for promoting fairness. These frameworks can act as a guide, outlining the bounds that AI systems must respect in order to maintain fairness. Developing procedures for tracking and assessing AI system performance—particularly with regard to fairness—becomes essential to these legal regimes. Furthermore, one of the most important aspects of the regulatory frameworks designed to advance fairness in AI is the provision of redressal channels—places where people can go to seek remedies for the negative effects of bias.

As we delve more into this area, it is important to emphasize how dynamic the pursuit of fairness is. AI is a field that is always changing as new innovations and breakthroughs appear quickly. As a result, in order to promote fairness, the methods and policies employed must also change and adapt to the rapidly evolving field of artificial intelligence. This calls for an ongoing dialogue about the subtleties of bias and an unrelenting search for tactics to promote fairness, negotiating the shifting landscapes with precision and vision.

By the time we get to the conclusion of this discussion, it should be clear that promoting fairness in AI is a deeply moral and social enterprise rather than just a technological one. It necessitates a team effort in which various organizations collaborate to negotiate the tricky paths between bias and fairness, creating avenues that lead to a just and equitable AI ecosystem. It invites a dedication to the values of justice and equity, creating an environment in which AI is used as a tool to improve human well-being rather than as a means of maintaining inequalities.

In conclusion, the discussion surrounding bias and fairness in artificial intelligence is a dynamic and developing field that requires a thorough and sophisticated approach to effectively manage its intricacies. At this critical juncture in human history, where AI has the potential to profoundly impact a multitude of areas of human endeavor, it becomes essential to confront bias and promote fairness. We set out on a journey towards a more just and equitable AI environment by means of a coordinated effort that includes a variety of techniques, such as examining data, promoting transparency, encouraging interdisciplinary collaboration, and creating regulatory frameworks. A future where AI acts as a force for good, promoting justice, equity, and well-being in the various tapestries that make up our global society, is what this journey is all about: constant learning and adaptation.

The challenge of interpretability

The story around interpretability in the ever-evolving field of artificial intelligence marks a major turning point in the continuous march towards the smooth integration of AI systems throughout human endeavors. The fundamental question of interpretability is how well humans are able to comprehend, rely on, and control the intricate calculations and decision-making processes that artificial intelligence (AI) systems do. Finding a balance between the complex functions of AI systems and the subtle aspects of human cognition depends on answering this question. In this section, we'll examine the diverse range of difficulties, factors, and initiatives related to AI interpretability, which is crucial to figuring out the technology's future course and social effects.

In the first part of our investigation, it is necessary to define interpretability in terms of AI dimensions. Artificial intelligence (AI) algorithms, particularly those that operate in the deep learning domain, frequently process layers of calculations, extracting patterns and subtleties from data in ways that may not necessarily make sense to human thinking. Due to their extreme complexity and multilayer structure, these algorithms frequently operate as "black boxes," with their inner workings remaining mysterious and difficult for humans to comprehend. This is a big problem because it makes it harder for AI systems to operate transparently, which is essential for building confidence and gaining traction.

The interpretation of the decision-making pathways of AI algorithms carries significant and genuine implications on multiple fronts, making it more than just a matter of limiting curiosity. For example, AI systems are increasingly being used in the healthcare industry to help with diagnosis and treatment planning. To guarantee safety and effectiveness in this case, medical practitioners' capacity to comprehend and verify the logic underlying AI-driven recommendations is essential. Similar to this, in the financial and legal spheres, promoting transparency and stopping unfair activities can be greatly aided by a knowledge of the underlying mechanics of AI judgments.

When we delve deeper, we discover that the problem of interpretability is complex and crosses societal, ethical, and technical boundaries. Technically speaking, the deep neural networks and complicated algorithmic architecture of contemporary AI systems provide an environment that makes it difficult to extract understandable insights. These systems frequently display mathematical and computational expertise that surpasses human understanding, causing a gap between the understandability of AI outputs and those of humans. To make matters worse, these algorithms frequently operate in high-dimensional, non-linear domains that are outside the scope of conventional explanatory frameworks.

The ethical concepts of responsibility and transparency are intimately linked to the problem of interpretability. When artificial intelligence (AI) systems are implemented in crucial domains like criminal justice or healthcare, their incapacity to analyze and comprehend the decision-making procedures may result in problems related to prejudice, discrimination, and accountability. In these kinds of situations, the inability to be interpreted clearly might impede efforts to maintain moral standards by making it challenging to examine and correct possible errors. Thus, the pursuit of interpretability is both a technological and an ethical imperative, guiding AI development in a direction consistent with the social ideals of accountability, transparency, and fairness.

The general public's trust and adoption of AI technologies are closely related to the interpretability difficulty in the social context. Since people may be hesitant to accept systems whose inner workings are opaque, the apparent opacity of AI systems could produce opposition and distrust. This situation may impede the wider adoption of AI in society, delaying advancement and the possible advantages that these technologies may offer. Therefore, solving the interpretability problem is essential to creating a society in which people view AI systems as trustworthy collaborators that support human pursuits rather than as mysterious entities that function in isolation.

As we investigate possible routes through these obstacles, we encounter a thriving ecosystem of initiatives and developments targeted at improving interpretability. On the one hand, scientists are attempting to create new techniques that will enable them to better understand the inner workings of artificial intelligence (AI) systems and remove their complexity. Promising advances in this direction include the methods of LIME (Local Interpretable Model-agnostic Explanations) and SHAP (Shapley Additive Explanations), which provide instruments for deconstructing and comprehending intricate AI models. Additionally, work is being done to create AI systems that can be understood by their own algorithms. In this way, transparency is promoted by the algorithms' ability to offer explanations in addition to their results.

Conversely, interdisciplinary approaches—which entail partnerships between experts in the fields of computer science, psychology, sociology, and other fields—are becoming increasingly effective in addressing the interpretability problem. These partnerships seek to create frameworks that can bridge the gap between AI systems and human cognition by fusing together knowledge from several domains. In addition, educational programs designed to improve the general public's comprehension of artificial intelligence and promote a critical thinking and inspection culture can be helpful in overcoming the interpretability problem. These initiatives are part of a larger movement to create a mutually trusting and understanding society in which AI systems and people may live side by side and work together.

The direction of AI development appears to be leaning toward a time when interpretability will be a key component. The increasing integration of AI systems into diverse domains of human endeavors is anticipated to raise expectations for clarity and comprehensibility. It is anticipated that regulatory frameworks and rules will also change, highlighting the importance of interpretability and creating an environment in which AI systems are created and implemented with a deliberate effort to uphold accountability and transparency.

In conclusion, the problem of interpretability in artificial intelligence is a dynamic and developing field that lies at the intersection of technological advancement, ethical concerns, and societal standards. As we traverse this complex terrain, encouraging a coordinated attempt to improve interpretability becomes imperative. With cooperative efforts, creative research, and a steadfast dedication to moral standards, we set out on a path to a day when artificial intelligence (AI) systems are transparent, ethically sound entities rather than mysterious "black boxes" that operate in opposition to society norms and human cognition. This is a journey marked by constant investigation and adaptation, leading to a point where the power of artificial intelligence is utilized in a transparent, mutually beneficial manner, thereby promoting a society in which technology acts as a beacon of development, equity, and well-being.

Technical challenges: Computation, storage, etc.

Over the past ten years, there has been an exponential increase in the development and application of AI and ML technologies, ushering in a new era of computational power that has the potential to fully transform a number of industries, including healthcare, finance, and education. These advancements have not, however, been made without a number of formidable technical challenges, most of which center on computational and storage capacities as well as related issues like energy usage, data handling, and network capabilities. This section explore the complex web of these issues, clarifying their various aspects and consequences for the advancement of artificial intelligence.

The need for extreme computational power is at the center of the AI revolution. In-depth AI models, especially those that deal with deep learning and neural networks, need a lot of processing power to handle and analyze massive amounts of data, find patterns, and produce informative results. This requirement results from the complex and frequently non-linear algorithms that form the basis of these models, where a large number of parameters and layers are involved and considerable processing power is required for both training and inference. Meeting these computing demands, however, is a huge undertaking that frequently pushes the bounds of current technology capabilities. More powerful options like Graphics Processing Units (GPUs) and Tensor Processing Units (TPUs), which provide parallel processing capabilities to speed computations, are becoming more popular as the more conventional Central Processing Units (CPUs) show signs of being unable to keep up with the computational requirements. However, creating and obtaining such sophisticated hardware infrastructures is an expensive endeavor that sometimes presents a challenge to small businesses and researchers with tight budgets.

Moreover, the computational difficulties also encompass the domains of energy usage. AI processes require a lot of electricity because they include intricate calculations and constant operation, which adds up to a significant energy consumption. With the large carbon footprint that comes with excessive energy use, this scenario not only comes with hefty operating costs but also raises environmental concerns. As a result, optimizing energy consumption through the development of energy-efficient hardware and algorithms becomes a crucial challenge in the current environment, coordinating the advancement of AI with sustainable development objectives.

The AI ecosystem is battling the issue of storage management concurrently. AI processes are data-centric, which means they must handle large datasets that are frequently high in volume, velocity, and diversity. Organizations must invest in strong storage systems that can handle the expanding data repositories without sacrificing performance or accessibility, which makes successfully storing and managing this data a major challenge. The difficulty of storage management is further compounded by the need to ensure data security and privacy, which calls for advanced encryption and access control measures to protect confidential data from breaches and unwanted access.

Furthermore, network capabilities and connectivity are essential parts of the AI infrastructure since they allow different parts of the system to communicate and transmit data. Ensuring high-speed connectivity to handle the data flow without creating bottlenecks and delays is the main problem here. With the promise of high bandwidth and low latency connections to simplify AI operations, the emergence of technologies like 5G and Fiber Optic Networks presents interesting options in this regard. However, the process of setting up and keeping up these network infrastructures is logistically and financially demanding, frequently necessitating large outlays and concerted efforts to be realized.

Through our exploration of this complex terrain of technological challenges, we encounter a thriving ecosystem of initiatives and developments targeted at overcoming these barriers. Research and development in quantum computing have the potential to completely transform computational capabilities by processing complicated AI algorithms at previously unheard-of speeds and efficiency. Additionally, work is being done to create neuromorphic computing systems, which offer powerful and energy-efficient processing abilities by simulating the functions of the human brain. These developments indicate possible avenues for bridging the computing divide and creating a setting in which AI operations can operate smoothly, faster, and with less energy usage.

Advances in cloud computing and edge computing present potential ways to address storage difficulties on the network and storage fronts. These technologies offer scalable and adaptable storage solutions that can adjust to changing data requirements. Moreover, decentralized and immutable data storage solutions that protect information from unwanted access and modification are made possible by the incorporation of blockchain technologies into data management. Furthermore, new developments in network technologies, such as Network Function Virtualization (or NFV) and Software-Defined Networking (or SDN), promise to improve network capabilities by providing flexible and agile network infrastructures that can meet the changing requirements of artificial intelligence operations.

Collaboration and interdisciplinary methods become effective solutions to overcome the technological challenges as we go through this changing terrain. Collaborations between researchers, policymakers, and industry participants create an environment that is favorable to innovation and makes it easier to combine resources and expertise to create all-encompassing solutions to the problems that are facing society. Additionally, interdisciplinary techniques, which combine knowledge from electrical engineering, material science, computer science, and other disciplines, promote a rich tapestry of innovation in which various aspects of the technical issues are approached from a variety of perspectives and specialties.

In conclusion, the path to an AI ecosystem that functions seamlessly is paved with a number of significant technical challenges, including those relating to computation, storage, and other aspects. These obstacles are major roadblocks in the way of AI's advancement and will require coordinated efforts and creative solutions to overcome. By means of cooperative efforts, scientific and technological advancements, and a dedication to ethical and sustainable practices, we set out to cultivate an AI environment that is not only powerful and effective but also compliant with the more general objectives of social advancement and ecological sustainability. Continuous research, adaptation, and innovation define this journey, which points towards a future where technical difficulties serve as stepping stones rather than obstacles and artificial intelligence (AI) shines as a lighthouse of efficiency, harmony, and progress in the digital age.

CHAPTER VIII

The Future of AI, ML, and DL

Emerging trends

Within the rapidly changing field of technology, the fields of Artificial Intelligence (AI), Machine Learning (ML), and Deep Learning (DL) are strong foundations supporting a period of revolutionary discoveries and methods. These dynamic areas are always changing, revealing fresher angles and patterns that are rerouting the course of technological advancement down less-traveled roads. Entering this exciting environment, we are met with a multitude of new developments that are changing the landscape of AI, ML, and DL and forming the shape of a future where technology should be more intelligent, integrative, and intuitive. This section explains some of the major developments driving this revolutionary path, creating a tapestry of innovations that will fundamentally alter both the technological and social landscapes.

The appearance of artificial general intelligence (or AGI) is a noteworthy trend in the field of artificial intelligence. Its objective is to create machines that possess cognitive capacities similar to those of humans. With this ambitious project, we hope to break through the limitations of narrow AI and create systems that are able to comprehend, learn, and do any intellectual work that a human can. This paradigm shift portends a time when artificial intelligence (AI) will be a creative and cooperative collaborator in a wide range of undertakings, including complicated decision-making processes and scientific research. The path to artificial general intelligence (AGI) is marked by unrelenting investigation and testing, utilizing developments in neurobiology, cognitive sciences, and computational technologies to create systems that emulate the complexities of the human brain and thus pave the way for previously unheard-of human-machine collaboration.

Concurrent with the advancements in Artificial Intelligence, the discipline of Machine Learning is experiencing a spike in trends that are challenging conventional methods. The introduction of federated learning, a unique paradigm that permits model training across numerous decentralized devices with local data samples without their exchange, is one such trend. This method improves privacy and security while making it easier to include a variety of data sources, which boosts the model's resilience and speed. Furthermore, learning to learn, or meta-learning, is becoming popular; in this approach, models are built to quickly adjust to new tasks using little or no data. This method makes use of the information gained from prior learning to speed up and improve the efficiency of learning in new domains, resulting in a more responsive and adaptive machine learning ecosystem.

Furthermore, the dynamics of model construction and deployment are changing due to the advancement of automated machine learning, or AutoML. By using automation to streamline the procedures of model selection, hyperparameter tuning, and data preprocessing, autoML helps to reduce the amount of time and skill needed to create effective machine learning models. This tendency points to a future in which machine learning (ML) will become more democratic and approachable, enabling people with little technical background to use ML to solve challenging issues and produce insightful findings.

A subfield of ML called deep learning is likewise going through a radical transition that is being marked by the introduction of new architectures and methodologies. One such invention that has transformed the field of natural language processing is the creation of transformer models. These models have demonstrated exceptional competence in comprehending and producing human language, which has led to breakthroughs in machine translation, text summarization, and sentiment analysis. They are distinguished by their capacity for parallelization and their attention mechanisms. In addition, the advancements in Generative Adversarial Networks (GANs) are propelling the Deep Learning (DL) field into novel frontiers. This allows for the production of high-quality, realistic synthetic data, which finds use in a variety of fields like as virtual reality, gaming, and the arts.

In parallel, the discipline of neuromorphic computing—which aims to create systems that replicate the functions of the human brain—is expanding into the domain of deep learning. This strategy makes use of the spiking neural network principles, which aim to mimic the neurobiological dynamics and topologies seen in biological neural networks. This paradigm promises to usher in a new era of powerful, energy-efficient computers that can complete difficult tasks with amazing precision and speed.

Furthermore, a rich ecosystem of cooperative innovation is being fostered by the fusion of AI, ML, and DL with other emerging technologies like blockchain, edge computing, and quantum computing. With the ability to execute intricate calculations at previously unheard-of speeds, quantum computing holds the potential to significantly increase computational capabilities, which will make it easier to solve challenging issues and optimize activities in AI and ML. However, edge computing makes it possible to process data closer to the source, which lowers latency and bandwidth consumption—two factors that are crucial for real-time artificial intelligence applications. Blockchain technology improves the security and privacy elements of AI operations by providing decentralized and secure data management solutions.

There is a growing emphasis on responsible and ethical AI as we navigate these exciting prospects. A growing body of knowledge and discussion around bias, fairness, and transparency in AI systems is encouraging efforts to create models that are not only technologically sophisticated but also consistent with moral and ethical standards. These initiatives aim to guarantee that the developments in AI, ML, and DL are applied for the benefit of society as a whole, promoting equality, justice, and inclusivity in the digital age.

In conclusion, new developments in the fields of AI, ML, and DL herald a period of revolutionary shift marked by breakthroughs that promise to push the limits of what is possible with technology. These trends—which range from the advancement of artificial general intelligence to its combination with quantum computing—are directing technological advancement toward a future in which artificial intelligence (AI) will hopefully be more than just a tool, but rather a cooperative partner that promotes advancement, creativity, and well-being. As we set out on this fascinating adventure, our aim should be to wisely use these trends, creating an ecosystem that is not just technologically sophisticated but also in line with the more general objectives of environmental sustainability and societal well-being. This is a collaborative innovation journey where technology, society, and environment all work together to shape a future where AI, ML, and DL come together to form a beacon of prosperity, harmony, and advancement in the digital era.

Potential societal impacts and considerations

These days, Artificial Intelligence (AI), Machine Learning (ML), and Deep Learning (DL) are pervasive in many aspects of society and have drastically changed the way we work, live, and engage with the world. While there are many advantages and opportunities associated with these technical breakthroughs, it is important to carefully assess any potential implications. AI, ML, and DL have a wide range of social effects that affect education, the economy, ethics, and the foundations of human civilization. In order to create a future that balances technical innovation with sustainability and human wellbeing, it is crucial that we carefully examine the possible societal implications and concerns that these technologies bring as we continue on this digital renaissance.

The first is that these technologies have significant economic ramifications. A new era of efficiency and automation has been brought about by the powerful tools of AI, ML, and DL. Businesses across various sectors are using these technologies to streamline operations, increase output, and promote creativity. The emergence of predictive analytics, autonomous vehicles, and smart manufacturing demonstrate the revolutionary potential of these technologies and point to an unprecedentedly convenient and efficient future. However, there are worries about job loss and growing economic inequities as a result of this automation rise. There is a real worry of job losses as computers take over repetitive and routine work, especially in industries where human labor is heavily used. Therefore, it calls for a proactive approach to education and workforce reskilling to make sure that people have the skills necessary to succeed in the new digital economy. In addition, in the AI-driven world, legislators and business executives must work together to develop an inclusive economic framework that reduces inequality and advances equal chances.

Concurrently, the moral implications related to the application of AI, ML, and DL are becoming more prominent. The growing use of these technologies in decision-making processes, whether in the legal system, healthcare industry, or financial sector, brings up important issues with accountability, fairness, and bias. Because artificial intelligence (AI) systems are human inventions, they are vulnerable to ingrained biases in the data they are taught on, which could reinforce preexisting inequalities and biases. Furthermore, serious issues with privacy and civil liberties are raised by the use of surveillance systems and facial recognition technology. Consequently, it is imperative to establish an ethical framework that oversees the creation and application of new technologies, guaranteeing that the tenets of accountability, transparency, and fairness are upheld. To create policies and rules that protect people's rights and dignity in the digital era, ethicists, technologists, and legislators must collaborate.

Education is one of the key industries that AI, ML, and DL are having a profound impact on. With the help of these technologies, personalized learning, predictive analytics, and intelligent tutoring systems are becoming possible and completely changing the face of education. Learning experiences can be customized by AI-driven educational systems to meet each student's unique needs and skill level, creating a welcoming and flexible learning environment. But this change also calls for a reconsideration of the educational curriculum and the role of instructors. The importance of the human touch—which is defined by empathy, comprehension, and guidance—increases when machines play a bigger part in education. In order to provide a holistic and stimulating learning environment, the educational system must change to promote a symbiotic interaction between technology and human expertise.

In addition, the fields of healthcare, urban planning, and environmental sustainability are all impacted by AI, ML, and DL. These technologies have demonstrated enormous promise in the healthcare industry for improving the precision of diagnoses, streamlining treatment regimens, and enabling telemedicine. Concerns about data privacy and the doctor-patient relationship are also raised by the growing reliance on AI-driven diagnostic technologies. Incorporating AI into smart urban planning requires cities to take inclusivity and sustainability into account, resulting in AI-driven urban landscapes that support harmonious, inclusive, and sustainable populations. AI and ML have the capacity to improve conservation efforts, resource management, and climate modeling in the context of environmental sustainability, resulting in a future that is in line with these objectives.

In conclusion, as we move deeper into the digital era, society will need to negotiate a wide range of opportunities and difficulties posed by the societal implications and considerations of AI, ML, and DL. Automation and innovation are the economic ramifications that present a new set of opportunities and difficulties that call for an inclusive and proactive strategy. The ethical implications of these technologies necessitate working together to create a framework that protects the values of accountability, transparency, and justice. Urban planning, healthcare, and education are among the industries going through revolutionary shifts that indicate a time when human knowledge and technology will coexist to promote development and well-being.

As we approach the dawn of a new era, the road ahead calls for cooperation and interdisciplinary thinking, promoting a conversation that unites technologists, legislators, ethicists, and the general public. It's a journey marked by purposeful innovation, where the application of AI, ML, and DL is dictated by larger objectives of sustainability and societal welfare in addition to the rules of technological advancement. The goal should be to create a future where technology and people coexist peacefully, utilizing AI, ML, and DL to create a more diverse, equitable, and harmonious society. This is a journey of exploration, where the potential of these technologies is used to weave a story of advancement that is in sync with the environment and human values, guiding us toward a time when technology acts as a lighthouse of creativity, optimism, and harmony in the constantly changing tapestry of human society.

New frontiers: Quantum computing and AI, AI in healthcare, etc.

In a world where technology is advancing rapidly, artificial intelligence (AI) keeps pushing the envelope and exploring new ground that could revolutionize a number of societal areas. The integration of AI with quantum computing and the broad use of AI in the healthcare industry are two such horizons that are noteworthy in this quest. These domains provide not just vast prospects but also complex obstacles that necessitate careful investigation and comprehension. When we explore these fields, we uncover a promising environment where knowledge, creativity, and technology come together to create new models for computation and healthcare.

With its promise of unheard-of processing power that can handle complicated problems that are currently beyond the capabilities of classical computers, quantum computing marks a paradigm shift in the field of computing. Quantum bits, or qubits, are used in quantum computers, which operate in compliance with the laws of quantum mechanics. Unlike classical bits, which can solely exist in one state at a time, qubits can exist in several states concurrently because of the phenomena known as superposition. This characteristic allows quantum computers to do complicated calculations at a rate that is exponentially faster than that of classical computers, along with quantum entanglement and quantum interference. This computational power combined with AI opens the door to a synergy that could transform the industry and greatly expand the capabilities of artificial intelligence.

Machine learning is one of the key areas where quantum computing has the potential to completely transform artificial intelligence. This is especially true for the computationally demanding task of training deep neural networks. The speed at which quantum computers can do parallel computations can be used to drastically cut down on the amount of time needed to train complicated models, which would quicken the pace of AI research and innovation. Additionally, quantum computing can improve AI's performance in modeling and optimization tasks, making it easier to solve challenging issues in a variety of industries, including banking, logistics, and drug discovery. For example, in the field of drug discovery, quantum computing can facilitate the very accurate simulation of molecular structures, hence accelerating the creation of novel medications and therapies. It is crucial to keep in mind that quantum computing is still in its early stages and that there are still numerous technological obstacles that need to be overcome. To fully utilize quantum computing in AI, major obstacles such as the creation of scalable quantum algorithms, error correction techniques, and stable qubits must be addressed.

However, the use of AI in healthcare is a sign of optimism for a new era in medical science that will be marked by efficiency, customization, and precision. Artificial Intelligence (AI) has the capacity to evaluate large volumes of data, which can help medical practitioners diagnose patients more quickly and accurately. Machine learning algorithms have the ability to precisely evaluate medical images, recognize trends, and find anomalies, which can help in the early diagnosis of diseases like cancer. AI can also aid in predictive analytics, which uses data to forecast when diseases may manifest, supporting preventive healthcare. Furthermore, the delivery of healthcare could be revolutionized and made more individualized and accessible through the integration of AI with wearable technology and telemedicine.

Wearables with AI capabilities, for example, can track a variety of health metrics in real-time, offering insightful information on a person's health and wellbeing. When combined with AI algorithms, these devices can anticipate possible health problems, allowing for prompt intervention and lessening the strain on healthcare systems. Furthermore, AI can be extremely helpful in the field of telemedicine by enabling remote monitoring and virtual consultations, which would help underprivileged and isolated areas receive healthcare. But there are also legal and ethical issues that arise when AI is used in healthcare. Informed permission, algorithmic bias, and data privacy are some of the issues that must be resolved to guarantee that the use of AI in healthcare complies with ethical and just standards. Furthermore, one crucial area that must be supported is the creation of AI algorithms that can collaborate with medical professionals, enhancing rather than substituting their skills.

Furthermore, the field of personalized medicine represents a promising prospect as AI continues to delve deeper into the healthcare industry. AI can make it easier to create individualized treatment programs that are particular to each patient's needs and genetic make-up by analyzing genetic data and other health-related criteria. With its potential to improve treatment outcomes and lessen unfavorable side effects, this strategy could usher in a new era of targeted and customized medical research. Furthermore, the combination of machines and artificial intelligence in surgery and rehabilitation offers intriguing prospects for improving the accuracy and effectiveness of medical operations.

In conclusion, the integration of quantum computing and wide-ranging applications in healthcare define the future frontiers of AI, which offer a landscape full of both potential and problems. Integrating AI and quantum computing holds great potential to transform the area, augmenting its functionalities and stimulating creativity. To fully realize the possibility of quantum computing in AI, however, rigorous research and teamwork are required to overcome the forthcoming technological obstacles. The application of AI in healthcare simultaneously ushers in a new era of precision, customization, and efficiency in medical science. However, there are also legal and ethical issues that must be resolved along the way, so proceed with caution and discernment.

Unlocking the potential of these interesting sectors will require a collaborative strategy that unites specialists from diverse disciplines and a commitment to ethical standards as we travel into these new frontiers. Exploration and discovery characterize the path ahead, where the convergence of knowledge, innovation, and technology promises to open up new avenues for healthcare and computation paradigms to be redefined, resulting in a more informed, healthier, and technologically advanced world. Through this journey, we hope to create a future where technology and human wellbeing are harmoniously shaped, leading us towards an infinitely bright future awaits.

CONCLUSION

Recap of key points

We have thoroughly examined a number of fundamental concepts and developing phenomena that are influencing the fields of AI, ML, and DL as we have journeyed through the complex tapestry that now represents these fields. As we come to a conclusion, it is appropriate to summarize the key ideas that represent the essence of our discussion in order to provide a brief summary of the richness of information that has been revealed throughout this in-depth investigation.

In the beginning, we explored the theoretical domains of artificial intelligence, presenting a clear image of its intricate yet fascinating terrain. By distinguishing between the capabilities and functions of narrow and general artificial intelligence, we laid the foundation for understanding the wide range of real-world applications of AI, which penetrate many different industries, transforming functionalities and promoting efficiencies. A large portion of our conversation was devoted to deciphering the mysteries of machine learning (ML), a branch of AI that emphasizes complex algorithms and computational techniques that enable machines to learn from experience. We broke down the three main categories of machine learning (ML): supervised, unsupervised, and reinforcement learning. Each type of ML adds something special to the system's capacity to identify patterns and reach conclusions.

Moving forward, our investigation led us to the brink of Deep Learning (DL), a more sophisticated area of machine learning. Here, we uncovered the layers of neural networks, the foundation of deep learning, which imitate the workings of the human brain and enable the creation of machines capable of learning and processing data at a never-before-seen depth. In this part, we looked at the different kinds of deep learning, such as Convolutional Neural Networks (or CNNs), Recurrent Neural Networks (or RNNs), and Generative Adversarial Networks (or GANs), which are the foundations of today's complex, data-driven applications.

We continued our journey by delving into the vibrant world of programming frameworks, which include TensorFlow, PyTorch, and Keras. These are essential tools that make it easier to create and implement AI and ML applications. We emphasized the need of choosing the appropriate tools for the job at hand, stressing the need for computational effectiveness and the vital role that high-quality data plays in creating reliable AI models. We discussed the nuances of data preprocessing and augmentation, clarifying techniques that improve data quality and support more precise and dependable AI models.

We also delved into the process of training AI models, illuminating elements such as loss optimization, cost functions, and strategies to avoid overfitting—a typical mistake in the machine learning space. We also explored pre-trained models and transfer learning, which enable learning process optimization at a reduced computing cost and time.

As the last part of our journey drew near, we dug into the ethical issues surrounding artificial intelligence, revealing the complexities of fairness and bias that are crucial in creating ethical AI systems. Our investigation did not hold back in bringing to light the technical and interpretability difficulties the field faces, with a focus on storage and computation problems that call for creative solutions.

In conclusion, we explored the new directions and possible social effects of AI, ML, and DL, imagining a time when these technologies will smoothly integrate with various industries, promoting progress and opening doors for ground-breaking discoveries. The final part of our discussion revealed the fascinating intersection of AI and quantum computing as well as the revolutionary role of AI in healthcare, indicating the start of a new era marked by efficiency, creativity, and previously unheard-of possibilities.

By the time we finish, it's clear that the fields of AI, ML, and DL are dynamic, ever-changing environments full of possibilities and potential that will change the face of the future and promote a technologically sophisticated, globally interconnected society. Our exploration of this terrain has been a rich and rewarding undertaking, revealing a world in which invention and technology come together to create a future full of limitless opportunities and exciting prospects.

Encouraging responsible and innovative use of AI

Artificial intelligence (AI) is a leading technical improvement that functions as a pioneer and a front-runner, redefining innovation and efficiency in a variety of industries. However, given the extraordinary growth we are experiencing at this time, it is our moral responsibility to promote an environment that values ethical and creative use of AI. It's a path paved with the values of morality, diversity, and vision, pointing to a time when technology will complement humanity rather than overtake it.

The demand for accountability in the use of AI systems first and foremost reflects the fundamental ideas of ethical conformance. It calls for the development of AI systems based on fairness and equity concepts rather than biases that can encourage inequality and discrimination. It also captures the need to stop AI from being misused to spread false information, which is an issue that has grown in the digital age. Therefore, it is imperative to develop AI systems that represent moral integrity, bringing technology achievements into line with the values of justice and human decency.

Encouraging the appropriate use of AI also emphasizes the necessity of accountability and transparency in its implementations. It advances the trend of developing systems that are comprehensible and interpretable, which encourages user confidence and dependability. It's an invitation to start conversations that break down the complex layers of artificial intelligence, providing insights into how it works and raising a critical user base capable of interacting critically with technology, so avoiding naive trust and encouraging a culture of critical engagement.

Moreover, the landscape of AI innovation is one of abundant possibilities and promise. This dynamic area combines creativity and technology to promote innovations that have the potential to transform a variety of industries, like healthcare, transportation, education, and entertainment. However, progress in this setting also necessitates a deliberate effort to lessen the negative effects of AI, such loss of jobs and breaches of privacy. It becomes a struggle to strike a balance between possible consequences and progress, creating avenues for innovation to flourish while preserving the core principles that characterize our community.

Furthermore, creating surroundings that are supportive of research and development—a place where ideas grow and creative solutions surface—is another aspect of promoting innovation. It denotes a dedication to training and education, giving the labor force the abilities and information required to traverse the challenging landscape of artificial intelligence. Additionally, it suggests the establishment of cooperative platforms where specialists from diverse domains come together to create interdisciplinary approaches to AI development, promoting a holistic growth trajectory that takes into account the many facets of the human experience.

In conclusion, the story of promoting ethical and creative applications of AI becomes complex and weaves together the themes of creativity, ethics, and the welfare of society. It is a call to action, asking all relevant parties—developers, legislators, and users—to join forces in an attempt to create an AI environment that reflects the values of accountability and creativity. It is a vision that looks beyond the boundaries of technical development, seeing a day when artificial intelligence (AI) will lead the human race toward a future marked by harmony, inclusivity, and unprecedented growth. By means of this cooperative and deliberate endeavor, we commence our quest to cultivate a technological renaissance, in which artificial intelligence (AI) serves as an exemplar of human resourcefulness and ethical accountability, paving the way for a more promising and fair future.

Thank you for buying and reading/listening to our book. If you found this book useful/helpful please take a few minutes and leave a review on the platform where you purchased our book. Your feedback matters greatly to us.

www.ingramcontent.com/pod-product-compliance
Lightning Source LLC
Chambersburg PA
CBHW052147070326
40689CB00050B/2408